Basic
Political Concepts

Basic Political Concepts

Alan Renwick and Ian Swinburn

Stanley Thornes (Publishers) Ltd

First published in 1980 by Hutchinson Education
Reprinted in 1981, 1982, 1983, 1984, 1986
Second edition 1987
Reprinted 1988

Reprinted in 1991 by
Stanley Thornes (Publishers) Ltd
Old Station Drive
Leckhampton
CHELTENHAM GL53 0DN
England

British Library Cataloguing in Publication Data
Renwick, Alan
    Basic political concepts. – 2nd ed.
    1. Political science
    I. Title   II. Swinburn, Ian
    320   JA66

ISBN 0 7487 0394 2

Typeset by Words & Pictures Ltd, Thornton Heath, Surrey
Printed and bound in Great Britain by
Courier International Ltd, Tiptree, Essex

To Sue and Marion

Contents

Acknowledgements

The Publisher's thanks are due to the following for permission to reproduce examination questions (pages 19, 37/8, 57/8, 78/9, 97/8, 109/110, 131/2, 157/8): The Associated Examining Board; University of Cambridge Local Examinations Syndicate; Joint Matriculation Board; University of London School Examinations Board; University of Oxford Delegacy of Local Examinations.

Foreword to second edition

Since publication of the first edition of *Basic Political Concepts* there has been increasing emphasis, by examination boards, on a conceptual approach to politics. This emphasis is now filtering down from A-level to the new GCSE syllabuses. A-level students are expected to be able to write with a degree of conceptual understanding that would have been unusual ten years ago. As before, the aim of this new edition is to enable students to develop both the framework within which to structure answers, and the level of analytical sophistication necessary for success at A-level.

This second edition retains the structure of the first, but we have taken the opportunity to update examples, expand the number of exercises and examination questions, and include new material where situations have changed considerably since 1980.

We hope that the new edition will prove as popular with staff and students as the first.

We would like to thank Basil Blackburn, Mike Winton, and the staff of the Norfolk College library for their help and assistance. Our thanks and love go to our wives and families for their forbearance during the preparation of the second edition.

Foreword to first edition

A conceptual approach to politics and government

Early formal studies in the classroom emphasize a factual approach. The student is busy sorting out and learning the basic facts about a particular area of study. The study of government is no exception to this. New examination syllabuses cover the necessary basic factual material. Students learn about the structure of political systems and the institutions which are part of the governmental process. A usual starting point is in those institutions which make laws, those which apply them and those which interpret them. Further, the officers who fulfil these functions are identified and their work described.

In Britain parliament is examined as the national law-making assembly. The structure of the organization is outlined, for example, it is a two chamber assembly and each chamber is further divided into the government and opposition benches. Also the process of law-making is reviewed and various officials, such as the Speaker, the Serjeant-at-Arms and Black Rod, are spotlighted for consideration.

Such foundation knowledge is important in itself, but also as a basis for advanced level study. At this level the objective is to train a student to analyse a political system, which in turn involves an examination of those ideas which underlie that system. Although the development of conceptual thinking has always been a feature of advanced studies, in recent years teachers and educationalists in Britain and America, most notably Jerome Bruner, have become increasingly concerned about the shortcomings of some traditional curricula in this respect. Robert Stradling relates this concern in his 'Notes for a spiral curriculum for developing political literacy':*

[Some traditional curricula fail] to provide students with the conceptual frameworks and cognitive apparatus for making sense of their world, coping with the information explosion and the consequent rapid and constant changes in the stock of knowledge, and interpreting new experiences.

In political education these observations have been noted and attempts have been made by educationalists and examination panels to incorporate a more direct conceptual approach in their work. Clearly an understanding of political concepts would help any citizen debate political issues more constructively, but for the politics student such understanding is vital.

According to Robert Stradling, concepts may be defined as 'general ideas representing classes or groups of people, things, actions and relationships which share certain characteristics'. In the following chapters a number of basic concepts will be mentioned, including order, power and authority. These and others are the key to a deeper understanding of institutions and procedures which have long been at the centre of A-level GCE courses in politics and government. There is a crucial relationship between political concepts and political institutions which should be noted early. The point is clearly made in notes issued by London University for the guidance of A-level teachers of the London syllabus.

The syllabus seeks to encourage teachers and candidates to see that, in a sense, institutions are themselves concepts (for example, what do we conceive Parliament as doing?) and that all institutions embody ideas and all ideas seek institutional form.

The British parliament is a well tried and tested institution of the state. Any analysis would involve an examination of the concepts which it has been created to embody. Parliament has supreme power to pass laws, which provide a framework of order in the observance of which progress can be made. The House of Commons itself makes real the principle of representation and elected representatives (Members of Parliament) are the personification of this ideal.

---

* Further details of titles mentioned throughout this book are contained in the Bibliography (page 161).

One of the major difficulties arising from a more conceptual approach is deciding which concepts are basic and which are more complex; which concepts are part of the substructure of a political system and which are part of the superstructure. What follows is an attempt to identify and define some basic concepts. More specifically the aim of each chapter is to unfold key concepts in a general way and then examine how they operate within the British political context. Successive chapters build upon what has gone before, so that the theme concept or concepts of a particular chapter will be linked to those previously explored. The final chapter deals with the important and complex concept of democracy. In building up a conceptual framework it is possible to compare and make distinctions in a more disciplined way and in addition it provides a means of coping with a wide range of material.

Some teachers may feel that the book lacks sufficient institutional material for it to be used as a textbook; in this criticism they would be justified. There are many perfectly adequate textbooks on the market, for instance *Introduction to British Politics* by Peter Madgwick, in which the student can find all the institutional information he needs. This book should be used in conjunction with such a text to explore some of the basic concepts which, we feel, are not always adequately covered in more traditional books.

It is the hope of the authors that this book may help the average A-level student to discover the value of a conceptual approach to politics.

1 What is politics?

One certainty about life is change; change from one season to the next, physical change as people age, and great sweeping social and economic changes which affect millions of people. It is also a basic need of man, in the midst of change, to seek security through predictability in order to survive, plan and develop. To a certain extent man achieves this through observing the patterns of the natural world and arranging human activities accordingly. It is in this way that the successful cultivation of crops is possible which in turn makes it possible to feed large numbers of people. Man is able to thrive on change if it is directed to his own benefit and it can be argued that societies which are too stable become stagnant and lacking purpose. So the kind of predictable patterns or patterns of **order*** sought by man are those which make change manageable and thereby contribute to his survival and well-being.

If change is a constant feature of man's world and the direction of change for the well-being of mankind is the usual pursuit of rational men, a further feature is **conflict** about what, when and how changes are to be made. Wherever men set themselves to a task there will be conflict. This conflict revolves not only around which goals to pursue, but also around the methods by which to achieve their goals. Conflict can range from mild verbal disagreement all the way to physical confrontation. The different aspirations, needs and values of individuals and groups is at the root of political activity. Such activity is to be found wherever people are engaged in making decisions on future change, a process which usually involves conflict. Politics, at its simplest, takes

* Words in bold type are defined in the Glossary on page 159.

place wherever conflict exists about goals and the method of achieving those goals. The process of solving conflicts, whether at home, in school, or at a national level, is a political process. Groups, individuals and nations may have different ideas about what type of change is necessary, how society should evolve, or how societies should relate to each other.

How, then, are these differences resolved? Who is best qualified to have the final word? There are many bases on which people and groups have claimed the right to decide. In many simple societies leadership is, or has been, associated with prowess in battle, in others leadership is associated with old age and wisdom and in most societies leadership has been associated with gender. Where differences exist the final word is left to those who have gained the **power** and **authority** to decide. In many cases this ultimate ability to decide resides with one person but in most cases there is also some form of advisory body to the leader. The person or group of people who make the final decisions have supreme power or **sovereignty**. In this way one begins to see a community organizing itself into a political system with laws, governmental institutions and conventions which facilitate the continued existence and survival of that community.

Those charged with governmental tasks make decisions which affect the life of all those in the community and there often grows up a division between the governors and the governed. There are many ways of viewing this division. To Marxists this division is based on class, with the ruling class maintaining their position by making decisions which keep the people under control. Others see liberal democracies like Britain, where there is competition between parties and participation by the mass in elections, as being societies where the division between governors and governed is bridged by a kind of invisible contract between the few that govern and the mass who follow. This contract is based on the governors constantly striving to improve the lot of the governed.

In many societies a major threat to stability arises when a leader departs the stage, whether naturally or through the conspiracy of others, and there is a need for a new leader. A number of William Shakespeare's plays are woven around the struggle for supreme power: *Julius Caesar*, *Coriolanus* and *Richard II*, for example. In many areas the process of leadership transition became formalized by the hereditary principle by which the reins of power were passed from father to son. The hereditary principle came to the fore in England early in its history and was largely accepted by the populace, who often linked the monarchy with spiritual as well as temporal power. Although the monarchs claimed sovereignty this was often disputed by pretenders to the throne or by rebellious nobles and, occasionally, rebellious peasants. There were always those who were ready to point to the abuses of power, the excesses of privilege and the weaknesses of monarchs.

As successive monarchs revealed their good and bad human characteristics, there grew a belief that more people should have the right to shape their own future. From the Magna Carta to the present day this involvement has been gradually won by the people of the United Kingdom. This evolutionary process has been largely peaceful. The English Civil War stands out because it was an unusual political event in England. The process of change has been marked by the gradual erosion of the royal prerogatives and the development of procedures to contain conflict within an institutional framework, most notably through a chamber of elected representatives – the House of Commons. As the right to vote became extended to more and more people, politicians began to seek a broad agreement or consensus of opinion to create the basis for legitimate political action.

According to the Liberal Democratic view of politics, this consensus as to the acceptable ways of carrying out political activity, though not necessarily over the goals of such activity, remains with us today. All the major political parties in Britain share a belief in, or a consensus on, the desirability of parliamentary government but the consensus does not extend to the types of policies to be pursued. For instance, the Labour Party – formed at the beginning of the twentieth century, to provide better representation for the working class – has always sought to achieve this object within the accepted political framework. It is often difficult to remember, when listening to politicians' speeches, that Britain's political stability relies heavily on shared ideas as to the importance of parliamentary democracy.

Not everybody would agree with this consensus view of political stability. Many would argue, as the Marxists do, that consensus is really only skin-deep. It is easy to have apparent consensus during times of plenty, but it is during times of real problems that the true class nature of the political system becomes apparent. In such times of crisis, for instance in Northern Ireland, governments resort to the use of force to enforce unpopular policies on many of the people. This ability to use force is, they argue, the real basis of government.

Left wing and right wing

Although often used these terms are of limited value in defining political dispositions. It must be remembered that they are terms that are relative to political systems rather than being absolute descriptions. A right-wing Russian communist, for instance, would be classed as being unacceptably left-wing in the USA. In the British context it is possible to represent political parties and their place in the spectrum, as in Figure 1 below.

Figure 1 *The distribution of political beliefs in Britain*

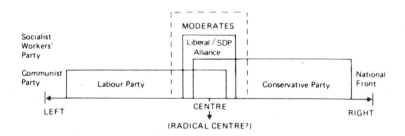

As Figure 1 indicates, each of the major parties embraces a broad spectrum of political opinion: the Labour Party from left to centre and the Conservative Party from right to centre. The Liberal/SDP Alliance occupies a central position, which has been said to be one of the reasons why it has found difficulty in 'breaking the mould' of the two-party system. Many potential Liberal/SDP voters are able to support some of the moderate policies put forward by the two major parties, and prefer to vote for one of the two major parties rather than 'waste' a vote on an alliance which has still to obtain complete electoral credibility. In the period since the formation of the Alliance in

1981 it has made some steps forward in this regard, but may still find it difficult in the future to maintain its momentum.

One striking feature of the British system is the lack of success of either extreme left-wing, or extreme right-wing parties. Consistently at elections such parties have failed to keep their deposits, let alone win seats. The National Front, Socialist Workers' Party and other such groups are weakened by the ability of the major parties to encompass wide-ranging political viewpoints. Extreme parties find it almost impossible to develop a strong enough power base in any constituency to take them close to success. The 'first past the post' electoral system ensures that they are unable to develop a power base in parliament which even approximates to their popularity in the country.

Since the end of the Second World War, government control has been successively in the hands of moderates of both parties – although the Thatcher government, elected in 1979 and re-elected in 1983, had a much more strident and right-wing flavour to it. As stated earlier the major parties share many of the assumptions about the acceptable ways of carrying out political activity, though not about the goals of such activity. It can be argued that since 1979 the gap between the parties, about what the goals of government should be, has increased to such an extent that it may no longer be possible to talk of consensus politics. Allowing for these changes it is still possible to say that all three major political groupings share a commitment to parliamentary democracy, a state welfare programme (although the scope of such a programme is a major source of disagreement between them), and a mixed economy which enables private and nationalized enterprises to exist side by side.

The Conservatives have placed much emphasis on encourage-ment of the private sector and the return to this sector of many previously state-run concerns: the so-called 'privatization' programme. They have supported private medicine, private schooling and have taken a strong line on law and order. In recent years there has been an increased emphasis on individual responsibility in both industry and personal life.

The Labour Party has concentrated on drawing basic indus-tries and services into public ownership and on managing the economy and planning its development. They emphasize the role of the government in helping those citizens who are in need by supplying a high level of public provision in Health, Education and Social Services. A long-term aim is the redistribution of wealth to create a more equal society.

In practice, neither party in government has been able to pursue and implement policies as fully as some of their more extreme members would like. This is partly due to practical difficulties and constraints but also has to do with the need to maintain public support in order to win elections. There is some evidence, however, that neither major political party is being successful in this latter aim; their core of dependable voters is declining. In recent elections the share of the total vote given to Labour and Conservatives has declined and this gives the Liberal/SDP Alliance its best hope of success. The process of partisan de-alignment which developed in the 1970s is thought to be the cause of the growing support for third parties. If the Liberal/SDP Alliance can gain an increasing proportion of these votes, it could break through the barrier of electoral success. To do this, though, it would need to convince the electorate that they have a viable set of policies, and this has proved a difficulty so far. The Alliance emphasizes the need to get away from the combative party system which leads to major swings of policy after General Elections and leads to opposition for the sake of opposition. It is in favour of electoral reform which would give a fairer representation of minority views in parliament. Proportional representation is a major priority for them. It favours the idea of partnership in industry rather than conflict, believing that the interests of managers and workers are similar. There are major disagreements within the Alliance, though, particularly about defence policy and specifically on the issue of unilateral disarmament. Whether the SDP in alliance with the Liberals can 'break the mould' of British politics remains to be seen.

The British political system has proved remarkably resistant to major change and there has never been a time when three major political groupings have co-existed. This resistance to change is at the same time a source of strength, since from it comes stability, and a source of weakness, for inertia builds up in the system limiting change when it is needed.

Essay question
1 What is politics? (Cambridge, Summer 1984)

2 Constitutions and constitutionality

What is a constitution?

Whenever groups of people gather together they develop sets of rules and principles by which they operate. Such rules and principles are at work in the home; parents tell their children how they expect them to behave and what principles govern such behaviour, for example: honesty, punctuality and good manners. Rules are possibly more important when one comes into contact with formal organizations like schools. In a classroom there are rules governing the relationships between the pupil and teacher, for example: there are rules on discipline and dress. More importantly perhaps there are customs which develop that are independent of the written rules; for instance, some teachers interpret the rules more strictly than others, some allow more informality than others.

Exercise
What are the major rules which govern your class? Are there any unwritten conventions which operate? Discuss your ideas with your teacher.

In some establishments with students' unions these rules, principles and conventions are written down in a formalized way. These rules outline the power of various officers and the procedures by which decisions should be made. Below is a part of a typical students' union constitution:

Union Representative Council
The Council shall serve for one academic year. Members of the Council shall be full-time class representatives, elected by ballot by the complete class, any other form of election shall be declared null and void. In the event of any position of class representative falling

vacant during the year the Committee shall take such action as it may deem necessary.

Each full-time class must be represented

Meetings of the Council shall be called by the Executive Committee

They will take place once a month during term-time

Notice of all meetings shall be given by the Honorary Secretary. Any Union member, part-time or otherwise, may be allowed to attend but unless he is a class representative is not allowed to take part in any proceedings unless asked to do so by an Executive Committee member. The duties of a class representative are:
(a) to speak on behalf of his class,
(b) to report Council meetings to his class.

An Emergency Meeting of the Council must be held within seven clear college days by the Secretary at the request of any one of the following:
(a) the President,
(b) the Executive Committee,
(c) one half of the members of the Council.

At least forty-eight hours' notice must be given to all members for an emergency meeting and the motion for adoption circulated.

At all meetings of the Council, one half of the total members shall form a quorum.

Discussion point
Is it necessary for any student union or school club to have such a formal set of rules? Could they operate solely on the basis of convention?

When we talk of a constitution we are usually thinking in terms of the constitution of a state, for example: the USA, the UK. A state is a group of people within a definite territorial boundary who have a set of shared beliefs and who are ruled by the same government. We have, now, the components for an answer to the question, 'What is a constitution?'

A **constitution** is composed of the principles, rules and conventions by which a state is governed. Constitutions normally outline the powers of the various parts of the governing body and the relationship which exists between various elements of the body. A consideration of the process of decision making and the rights of the individual are also elements. Some of the elements are likely to be formally set

down, but many are likely to be the product of tradition and
necessity and convention.

Types of constitution

Unfortunately the position is not quite as straightforward as
the above definition implies, different political systems have
come to different constitutional arrangements and it is
necessary to try to clarify constitutions in some way. The most
usual way is to take contrasting sets of terms, for example:
(*a*)   written/unwritten
(*b*)   flexible/rigid
(*c*)   unitary/federal
We shall follow this accepted pattern but would point out that
it is best to see these terms as what the sociologists would call
'ideal types'. An ideal type is an analytical tool to show the
purest form of a phenomenon, as the explanation is taken to
extremes it is unlikely that it will be encountered in the real
world. It is probably best to think of these terms as
representing the extremes of a line. Along the line could be
ranged all constitutions, for example:

Written	USA	GB	*Unwritten*

This approach implies that more of the US Constitution is
written down than the UK Constitution. It is, however, a
common error to say that 'The British Constitution is
unwritten'. We shall now see that this is only partially true.

Written and unwritten constitutions

A *written constitution* is one which can be found in a single
document which outlines the constitutional structure and
arrangement within a state – a *codified* constitution.

An *unwritten constitution* is one where various elements
may be written down but there is no one single document
which outlines the constitution of the state – an *uncodified*
constitution.

The British Constitution is classified as unwritten whereas
most other countries have written constitutions. It is mainly
a product of historical chance which, so far, has enabled

Britain to do without a written constitution. There has been little need for the total rethink of government which would be implied by the adoption of a written constitution, although the demand for one is growing as people become increasingly worried about the growth of large organizations, including government departments and public corporations, in relation to individual democratic rights. There has been much debate about the need for a written constitution in the UK, including the contributions of Sir Leslie Scarman's Hamlyn Lectures (1974) and Lord Hailsham's Dimbleby Lecture (1975).

Many countries that have written constitutions required them after a major conflict or change, in order to make a new start. The American Constitution was adopted after the War of Independence from the United Kingdom. The West German Basic Law was adopted after the Second World War and so was the Japanese Constitution.

Activity
Many embassies have education sections which are willing to provide copies of constitutions and details of political systems. As a class, find the addresses of some embassies and write for this information. Do the constitutions have any similarities?

Sources of the British Constitution

Britain has had no such major upheaval since the 'Glorious Revolution' of 1688 when James II fled the country and was replaced on the throne by William and Mary. Our political system has been stable and has evolved gradually. Unfortunately for the student of politics this has meant that a simple account of the sources of the constitution is difficult. There are a number of sources which contribute elements to our constitution but no simple authoritative document. The main sources are generally thought to be:

1 Constitutional documents
Some documents have become the foundations of our constitution because they express important constitutional principles. Magna Carta of 1215 asserted the principle that a monarch could and should be controlled by his subjects. Other

important documents include the Bill of Rights of 1688, which limited the Royal Prerogatives (privileges) and the Act of Settlement of 1701, which further strengthened parliament's control over the sovereign of the country by controlling succession to the throne.

2 Major statutes
Not all statutes embody principles which affect the constitutional structure of the country but some have important and often obvious effects, because they materially alter the way in which we are governed or the relationships within the state. Some recent examples are the Parliament Acts 1911 and 1949, the Representation of the People Act 1969, and the Local Government Act of 1985 which abolished the Greater London Council and the Metropolitan County Councils.

3 Constitutional conventions
As we have seen, all political systems develop conventions to aid their smooth running. Britain, with no codified (written) constitution has developed an enormous range of conventions which have come about to fulfil certain needs. There are too many conventions to attempt to list anything but a sample. These include:
(a) The office of Prime Minister and cabinet government have emerged through need and have remained by convention.
(b) The monarch calling the leader of the majority party to be Prime Minister after a general election, and after receiving the resignation of his predecessor.
(c) The non-partisan nature of the monarchy. As head of state, the monarch is traditionally held to be above politics, a situation which facilitates stability and continuity.

Exercise
From your library discover three other conventions (most books on British government should have a list). Why are these conventions useful? What would happen if they were broken?

4   *Case law*

Case law is sometimes called 'judge made' law because it is the result of judges' decisions which affect the constitution. Although the judiciary is largely non-political in Britain it does interpret statutes which may be unclear, in addition it often establishes individual rights in relation to authority. An interesting example which affects the working of the legal system itself occurred in 1986. The Law Lords ruled that magistrates were liable for damages if suits were successfully brought against them. Previously it had been thought that magistrates, like judges, were immune from damage suits.

5   *Major political works and writers*

Because of the complex nature of the British Constitution the works of certain authors interpreting the constitution have become part of the constitution itself. These works often contain the nearest to a written account, of the way the constitution operates, that we possess. Works such as *Treatise on the Law, Privileges, Proceedings and Usage of Parliament*, Erskine May (1844), *The English Constitution*, Walter Bagehot (1867) and *Law of the Constitution*, A.V. Dicey (1885), have become standard works.

It is clear, then, that most of these elements are written but not simply contained in one place. Those countries which have written constitutions may also have difficulties outlining their constitutions at any stage. The USA for instance, has many features not mentioned in the constitution, for example, political parties and pressure groups which must obviously be taken as part of the constitutional structure. Equally, the constitution itself is constantly being reinterpreted by the participants in the political struggle.

When talking of written and unwritten constitutions, we must be aware that all countries have both written and unwritten elements within their constitutional structure. The terms 'written' and 'unwritten' must be taken as an indication of the formality of these elements.

Rigid and flexible constitutions

We can give a working definition of these two terms: this will help us to begin our analysis but should be taken to be provisional and open to change.

A *flexible constitution* is one which can change without any lengthy or difficult process.

A *rigid constitution* is one which requires some lengthy or difficult process to alter it. Such a process is usually outlined in the constitution itself.

The generalization is often made that the British Constitution is flexible, after all, it is in a constant state of change – this makes it difficult to pin down at any stage. The process by which the constitution gradually alters cannot be easily explained: it is the result of the diffuse nature of the constitution outlined previously. The lack of one written constitutional statement means that any of the other sources dealt with can change. Broadly, though, it is possible to outline the usual types of circumstances which cause each of the elements to change.

Conventions, those indispensable customs of political practice, change in response to new circumstances and reinterpretation of the existing conventions. A good example would be the continuing change in the doctrine of individual and collective responsibility. The usual way to explain these is to say that collective responsibility imposes on ministers the duty to agree in public with cabinet decisions, even if they disagree personally with them. If they cannot do this they should resign. However, in recent administrations there has been a slackening of this convention and more cabinet ministers disagree publicly with cabinet decisions.

Although the Conservative Government under Mrs Thatcher attempted to reinforce the traditional notions of collective responsibility, this was not without some difficulty. The open cabinet disagreement between Mr Michael Heseltine and Mrs Thatcher over the Westland Helicopter Affair of late-1985 and early-1986 led eventually to the resignation of Mr Heseltine, but not until the end of an acrimonious public debate.

Individual responsibility is explained as ministers being responsible for all actions of their departments' civil servants, whether they authorized such action or not. At times it has even been applied to actions of the department before the

minister was in charge. An example is the Crichel Down Affair
of 1954, where Sir Thomas Dugdale resigned as Minister of
Agriculture.

This convention appears to have been modified in recent
years so that a minister would only be expected to resign if
he or she had direct knowledge of maladministration or
incompetence, or if a major decision made by themselves is
subsequently proved to be badly flawed. In April 1982 Lord
Carrington, Mr Humphrey Atkins and Mr Richard Luce
resigned from their posts at the Foreign and Commonwealth
Office as a result of the Argentine invasion of the Falklands
Island. Lord Carrington's letter of resignation said, in part:

> The Argentine invasion of the Falklands Islands has led to strong
> criticism in Parliament and in the press of the Government's policy.
> In my view, much of the criticism is unfounded. But I have been
> responsible for the conduct of that policy and I think it right that
> I should resign.

Constitutional documents, by their nature, lead to change
slowly. Once a document has acquired such status it tends to
retain it for many years. As a result this is probably the one
element in the British Constitution which remains relatively
static. The same cannot be said for *constitutional statutes*;
these are important laws which affect our constitution. It
should be remembered, though, that most laws cannot be
considered as part of our constitution, except in the most
peripheral way. Statutes of constitutional importance require
the same legislative programme as any ordinary Act of
Parliament and often their passage can be carried out quickly.
Some acts of importance include the 1911 Parliament Act
curbing the power of the Lords, and the 1918 Representation
of the People Act extending the vote to women over thirty
years old.

Case law can alter with a judge's interpretation of laws. The
1979 decision by the Law Lords that the law of blasphemous
libel was still operable, after the publication by *Gay News* of a
poem about Jesus Christ, reimposed a limit on freedom of
expression which many thought to be defunct.

Major political works and treatises acquire this status when
they add to our existing knowledge of the constitution or
reinterpret it. Richard Crossman's *Diaries* may become a

major work in this respect, but may remain too personal to acquire the status. His introduction to *The English Constitution* by Bagehot is now accepted as a major outline of the constitution. It should be noted that accepted works like Erskine May's have long since ceased to have their original form but provide a wealth of reference material on the nature of the constitution at present.

Although the British Constitution is flexible and is changed to meet new needs, there are certain constitutional principles and ideas which are unlikely to alter because they are central to the British system of government. Any government trying to change them would have difficulty in being re-elected.

The USA is often compared with the UK and said to have a rigid constitution. Article 5 of the United States Constitution lays down rules for amendments and states that:

The Congress, whenever two-thirds of both Houses shall deem it necessary, shall propose amendments to this Constitution or, on the application of the Legislatures of two-thirds of the several States, shall call a convention for proposing amendments, which, in either case, shall be valid to all intents and purposes, as part of this Constitution, when ratified by the Legislatures of three-fourths of the several States, or by conventions in three-fourths thereof, as the one or the other mode of ratification may be proposed by the Congress.

Such a procedure is obviously difficult and time-consuming. Only twenty-six amendments have been ratified since 1786. Although classified as rigid, the US Constitution has a degree of flexibility which surprises many people. Parties and pressure groups have no formal constitutional position and yet are part of the constitutional framework of the US. The Supreme Court's ability to interpret the constitution provides for greater flexibility. However, it is the power of the President that provides the clearest example of constitutional flexibility. Originally the framers of the US Constitution foresaw a fairly minor role for the President but he has become the most powerful man in the world. How? His powers are set out in a vague manner in the US Constitution and he has been able to extend them as the power of the federal government has extended. This has necessitated no constitutional changes but has led to the President being the major instigator of legislation, the focal point of the nation and, to an extent, economic supremo.

All written constitutions depend upon interpretation. The US has looked on the word of the constitution as sacred but at the same time it has been willing to interpret the word freely.

The intention of this section has been to show that 'rigid' and 'flexible' are relative, not absolute, terms. When used with care they are useful concepts, if taken too literally this can obscure much of the truth.

Unitary and federal constitutions

All states face the problem of where final power should reside, which unit or units within the system should be supreme. There are two basic solutions to the problem: to have one **sovereign** body which is all-powerful; or to have many small bodies which are presided over by a limited central authority. The first solution is that taken by unitary states such as Britain, the second by federal states such as the USA and the USSR. Figure 2 represents this diagrammatically.

Figure 2 *Unitary and federal government*

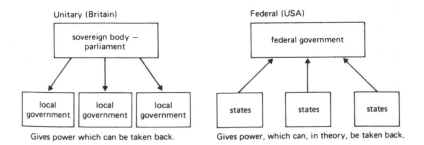

It is clear from this that in Britain parliament has the power to make or unmake laws, to delegate powers and to control other governmental units, for example, local government. This absolute sovereignty of parliament is limited in practice by a number of factors which we will explore later. In the USA, several states joined together for their common defence, and gave up some of their powers to a federal government in return for its protection. In many federal countries, theoretically, each member state has the option to withdraw from the federation but this is, in practice, almost impossible because of the growth of power of federal governments. The unsuccessful attempt by Biafra to withdraw from the Nigerian Federation in May 1967, is a case in point.

We will return to the problem of distribution of power within the nation-state when exploring the need for a federal Britain and the limits to the sovereignty of parliament.

These three sets of terms, then, are most often used as a shorthand for describing constitutions, but one must remain aware of their simplification. Nevertheless, we can generalize and say that Britain exemplifies an unwritten, flexible and unitary constitution while many other countries, for example, the USA, Germany and the USSR, have written, rigid and federal constitutions.

Constitutionality

The constitution of most countries embodies the principles by which that country should be governed, but governments and individuals do not always act in a constitutional way. Many dictatorial regimes violate human rights even when these are specifically mentioned in their constitution. In some countries government is constitutional in that political leaders try to act within the framework established by the constitution: but even so, cases of unconstitutional behaviour by governments do occur, and these cases must be dealt with. In countries which possess a written constitution it is common for a supreme court to exist. Such a court interprets the constitution and makes judgements upon the constitutionality of certain actions. The United Kingdom does not, however, possess such a court, relying instead on the ordinary legal process and parliamentary control of government.

The lack of a supreme court in Britain has led many people to argue that civil and political rights are open to abuse by any government that is willing to act in an unconstitutional way. In Northern Ireland, there have been cases of torture of prisoners and cases where basic rights have been neglected. The Prevention of Terrorism Act enables the police to hold people without charge for longer than is normally acceptable, and on different grounds to those held on normal charges. Because of the flexible nature of the British Constitution the Prevention of Terrorism Act is constitutional. We have no Bill of Rights which sets down our individual rights that cannot be removed by a sovereign parliament.

Despite lapses, it is clear that British governments and other organizations in society abide by the constitution. There does, however, seem to be a growing anti-constitutional trend. This means that there are individuals or groups who want to replace the existing constitution by another. Such attitudes are clearest in extreme groups such as the Irish Republican Army (IRA), who do not want to change the constitution but to replace the present constitutional structure by a new one based on a united Ireland. This activity threatens the existing constitutional arrangements and so is opposed by those who support the status quo. In Britain it is not unconstitutional to advocate the overhaul of the present system but it becomes illegal when criminal actions are used. Not all constitutional changes takes place on such an extreme level. It is difficult to see, on occasions, whether a party is working for massive reforms of the constitution or the adoption of a new one.

The Liberal Party provide an example. In their 1983 election manifesto, they reaffirmed their belief in parliamentary government but agreed that major constitutional changes were necessary. Among their proposals were:

(*a*)   Electoral reform to improve democracy
(*b*)   A Freedom of Information Bill on US lines to allow automatic public access to information unless such access is against the national interest
(*c*)   Fixed parliamentary terms
(*d*)   Decentralization of government to Scotland, Wales and the English regions.

These proposals suggest major constitutional changes, but they cannot be seen as anti-constitutional in that those who support their implementation confine themselves to legally acceptable methods. To sum up we can say that:

(*a*)   *Constitutional government* occurs when government activity and that of individuals upholds the constitution and acts within it.
(*b*)   *Unconstitutional actions* are those which break the

constitution, whether in a major or minor way.
(c) *Anti-constitutional actions* are those which attempt to
destroy a constitution, normally replacing it by another
system.

Exercise
Most governments place restrictions on those people who
seek to destroy their constitution. What justifications are
there for such restrictions?

Constitutional principles in Britain

It is difficult to isolate the major constitutional principles of an
unwritten constitution, especially when those principles have
to be greatly qualified. Bearing this in mind, there seem to
be three major constitutional principles which are important
in Britain:
(a)   The sovereignty of parliament
(b)   The supremacy of law (or the rule of law)
(c)   The separation of powers.

The sovereignty of parliament
The British parliament is the supreme body within the United
Kingdom. It has the power to make and unmake any law it
desires without any non-parliamentary body being able to
control its decisions. Put at its simplest this is the doctrine of
'the sovereignty of parliament'. On the face of it, the doctrine
seems to be a realistic one: only parliament can pass laws and
only on its authority can government action be taken, but
there are many limits to the actions which parliament has at its
disposal. Freedom of action is limited by (among other things):

1   *The need to gain public support in elections*
Political parties try to promote their political manifestos in a
pre-election campaign in order to gain a majority in the House
of Commons.

2   *The need to ensure continuing public support for policies*
No government can afford to lose too much support, hence
unpopular measures tend to be implemented in the early
stages of an administration's five-year term. A television

broadcast by a Prime Minister informs the public of a major problem facing the government and the measures to be adopted to solve it. The intention is to gain support, through explanation, for what are likely to be rather stiff remedies. Prime ministers throughout the 1970s and 1980s attempted to rally national support for anti-inflationary measures in this way.

3 The European Economic Community
By the signing of the Treaty of Rome, a degree of British sovereignty was passed to the European Community.

4 International financial organizations
The International Monetary Fund, for example, imposes conditions on loans and financial aid granted. This may restrict the freedom of action of a Chancellor of the Exchequer in devising budgetary measures; such was the experience of Mr Denis Healey in 1976.

5 Other international bodies
Membership of the North Atlantic Treaty Organization (NATO) means that in return for the security afforded by an international military alliance, certain obligations have to be accepted. Britain would be bound to respond if an aggressor attacked another member country, even though she might not be directly involved in the first instance.

6 Powerful groups in society external to government
Successive governments have become increasingly aware of the need to carry powerful groups in society if policies are to be applied successfully. For instance, both Mr Harold Wilson and Mr Edward Heath, during their terms of office, maintained regular dialogue with TUC and CBI representatives on crucial aspects of industrial and economic policy. Mrs Thatcher has not encouraged such dialogue.

The sovereignty of parliament is limited in practice by the nature of the British political system: in a democratic nation the people are sovereign. Their wishes must ultimately control government and parliament and so their support is essential. Britain can no longer be seen as an island, her links with external bodies are too strong; without external links Britain could not survive. Their ability to place some controls on the British political system is the price of membership of the international community.

The supremacy of law (rule of law)

One major determinant of the constitutionality of a government is the extent to which it operates within the framework of the law produced by the legislature. In the Western democracies legality is held to be the ultimate justification for an action, both for governments and the individual. Any individual who breaks a law can expect to be held accountable for his actions. In this way the law deters undesirable behaviour. Governments must also act within the law or else face the penalties for breaking the law. They are not above the law even though they often have the power to create, or at least influence the creation of, laws.

The rule of law implies that the law applies equally to all within a society and that governments as well as individuals are subject to the constraints of the law. As with the sovereignty of parliament, the principle can be overstated in relation to practice in Britain, for the law is not equally accessible to all and is not applied equally to all. Social status, education and wealth count considerably when legal proceedings are a possibility. Litigation is a costly affair, therefore powerful and wealthy individuals and groups have a natural advantage in gaining redress for grievances, though this has been offset by the introduction of legal aid and the work of tribunals. Although government departments and large corporations do have built-in advantages, they do not always win in court. The dispute of 1975 between the Tameside Council and the Minister of Education over compulsory comprehensivization showed that it was possible for the government to lose a legal case (although it also showed that the government then has the power to change the rules of the fight so that it eventually wins). It is less rare for the government to lose cases in the European Court of Human Rights, the British government having notable setbacks on the issues of telephone-tapping and the use of corporal punishment in schools.

Certain individuals have more legal rights than, or are

treated by the legal system in a different way from, the ordinary citizen. A football fan carrying a pickaxe handle is likely to be arrested for carrying an offensive weapon by a policeman who is carrying a truncheon. More worrying, perhaps, is the ability of certain individuals or groups to break the law without, apparently, facing the consequences. There is considerable evidence that many people involved in white-collar crime go undetected and therefore unprosecuted. Two possible reasons for this are the complexities associated with uncovering this type of crime, and the high status of those involved. There is also the unfortunate way in which some public figures facing trial may be subjected to a process of 'Trial by Media' which, even if it does not affect the outcome of the trial, often has an adverse effect on careers. The case of Jeremy Thorpe and his trial in 1979, on conspiracy to murder charges, of which he was acquitted, may be a case in point.

Although acquitted of the charges against him, Mr Thorpe withdrew from public life, largely as a result of the adverse publicity the case produced. His personal life, and particularly the allegations of homosexuality, became the subject of media attention to such a degree that he felt he could no longer continue to work in public life.

Discussion point
Should any person or group be above the law? Which groups need to be given special rights?

The application of law to all is protected by the independence of the judiciary. Once appointed, a judge is largely free from political pressure and can only be removed in exceptional circumstances. Judges, however, can only interpret existing laws and enforce the penalties of the law; they cannot create or influence laws (except, of course, case law). Nor can they, as in some countries, judge that a law is contrary to the constitution. They can, however, ensure that no person is punished without the legal process having taken its course. There is no arbitrary imprisonment in the UK during normal peacetime.

The separation of powers
The independence of the judiciary (and hence, the rule of law) is helped by the separation of powers. All political systems

need to perform three basic tasks to operate effectively. Therefore, there need to be 'three arms of government': the legislature, executive and judiciary.

The *legislature* creates laws (in Britain this is the task of parliament).

The *executive* puts the law into effect (in Britain this is the task of government).

The *judiciary* judges in cases of dispute, or where the law has possibly been broken (in Britain this is the function of the court system).

Ever since Montesquieu (1689–1755), a French philosopher, attributed Britain's moderate government to the separation of the three arms of government, it has been thought that moderate government relies on no one person or group being able to control all three arms. He argued that each arm is able to exert control over the others and thus moderate it. His theory had considerable influence on the founding fathers of the US Constitution, who purposely instituted checks and balances throughout the US political system.

Ironically, Montesquieu over-emphasized the extent to which the powers were separate in Britain, since there is, in practice, considerable overlap between them.

The Lord Chancellor, for instance, is a member of all three arms of government in his role as a cabinet minister (executive), speaker of the House of Lords (legislative) and head of the legal system (judicial). Parliament exercises some judicial functions – the House of Lords is the highest court of appeal and all members of the executive are also members of the legislature.

Exercise
Figure 3 shows two diagrams: the first, Montesquieu's theoretical separation of power; the second, a more accurate representation. Try to find out which individual or group forms the overlaps.

Conclusion

To see constitutions as being fixed or immovable objects is to misunderstand their true nature. It is perhaps more accurate to think of them as organisms that change and mature, in some

Figure 3 *The separation of power*

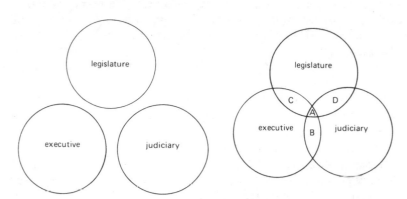

cases even decay. The British Constitution, because of its diffuse character, is almost impossible to describe accurately at any point in time, as the elements within the constitution change and those that remain constant are of differing levels of importance at different times.

As the process of growth and debate continues, many are calling now for more open government based on greater access to information. Such a move would greatly affect the constitution, especially as such a demand is often linked to the call for greater protection for the individual through a Bill of Rights. Meanwhile, some constitutional problems diminish in importance; devolution, which before the 1979 referendum was a major political issue, has now ceased to have a great impact on the public.

Essay questions
1 'Britain does not have a written constitution, but it does have both statutes and conventions which do the job just as well.' Discuss. (Oxford, Summer 1983)
2 What advantages and disadvantages would follow from the introduction of a written constitution in Britain? (Cambridge, Summer 1982)
3 How is the constitution changed in Britain? Illustrate your answer with examples drawn from this century. (London, June 1981)

4   'Far from being flexible, the British Constitution is
     exceptionally rigid.' Discuss. (London, January 1982)
5   'The British Constitution itself is now an object of political
     dispute.' Discuss. (London, January 1985)
6   Have some recent disputes indicated the need for a
     written constitution? (London, June 1986)

Short-answer questions

1   State three major conventions of the British Constitution.
     (London, January 1981)
2   What would constitute an unconstitutional action on the
     part of a government? (London, June 1981)
3   Give examples of anti-constitutional groups in Britain.
     (London, January 1983)
4   Give examples of anti-constitutional activity. (London,
     June 1985)
5   Define 'rigid' and 'flexible' in relation to constitutions.
     (London, January 1985)
6   What is meant by 'sovereignty'? (London, June 1985)
7   What is meant by 'a constitution'? (London, January
     1986)
8   What is meant by 'collective responsibility'? (London,
     January 1986)
9   Define 'constitutionalism'. (London, June 1986)

3 Order and disorder

Professor Bernard Crick has provided these definitions of order and disorder. Order is:

the most general perception that rational expectations about political, social and economic relationships, almost whatever they are, will be fulfilled. Disorder is when one does not know what is going to happen next, or more strictly when uncertainties are so numerous as to make rational premeditation or calculation appear impossible.

Order is fundamental to existence. Human beings can only survive by following patterns of order in the physical world. In this way human needs and some human desires can be fulfilled. Early man as a gatherer and hunter not only learnt which berries were edible and when they were ripe enough to eat, but also became skilled at catching animals and fish. Eventually men became settled cultivators of the land and by observing the order of the seasons were able to choose the right times to sow, cultivate and harvest.

We are all dependent upon order in our everyday life. The properties of certain materials and the way they are structured into certain forms must be understood. Wood has the quality of hardness and when constructed into a chair is intended to bear the weight of a person. A man who knows these facts is able to sit on a chair assuming that the wood has been so arranged that it will take his weight.

A person planning a journey depends on an organized system of transport. The times of buses and trains are important to know if successful plans are to be made.

The thoughtful student soon realizes the necessity of an organized approach to study and a well-ordered file of material to revise from before examination day.

Exercise

Make a timetable of an average day. How many of the activities you undertake depend upon your assuming that patterns which have occurred will be repeated? What would happen if such patterns disappeared?

It is clear that order is essential to survival, but it is more – it is essential to change. Within any political system there is an impetus to survive and progress within a framework of order. All political systems apply some kind of order. Order can be effective, in the sense of creating regularities, but may be unjust, in that it denies citizens rights. If effectiveness is the main criterion for a successful application of order then perhaps the late General Franco's dictatorship in Spain would be placed high on the list. Franco created a highly ordered society but one in which political opposition was stifled and citizens strictly controlled. Furthermore, liberal democracies must accept some elements of *disorder* if an acceptable system of **order** is to be applied.

Responses to law and order

In the previous chapter the marking out of power and authority according to a constitution has provided some insight into the way political order is created and maintained. It is important now to examine the nature of political order and how it may break down in certain circumstances.

Government officials who make decisions receive various responses to those decisions from members of the community.

Compliance

This response by a majority of citizens provides a basis for order. By definition, **compliance** involves submission by a person to the commands of those who govern. A person may be half-hearted or totally disagree with the commands but obey because he fears the consequences of not doing so. A government can continue because it is able to exercise power even though conformity to the existing pattern of order by the mass of the population is involuntary. Compliance is all that is usually achieved by dictators and autocrats for they rule through fear. A dictator controls armed forces, the civilian and secret police, and through these is able to dispose of opposition by individuals or groups within society. Usually the threat of physical violence is sufficient to keep the majority of people compliant. This was the way of Adolf Hitler in Nazi Germany and more recently of Idi Amin in Uganda. For a dictator who governs in this way there are inherent weaknesses for he can never be sure that he has the support of even a minority of people in his country. There is always the fear that beneath the appearance of order there may be deep opposition to authority which may erupt into violent disorder at any time.

Consent
As with compliance, this response by the majority of citizens makes for order within a society. **Consent** may be defined as the agreement of the majority of the populace to accept and live by the decisions made by those who govern. Unlike **compliance, consent** involves agreement by most people that leaders emerge through a legitimate process. Such consent is more visible in liberal–democratic societies such as those that exist in Western Europe and the United States, in which political machinery exists for an electorate to choose from different programmes of change presented by different political parties. Moreover, institutions are established to check the work of the government on behalf of the voters. At the national level, parliament fulfils this function in Britain and Congress in the USA. Consent tends to be given more readily because the electorate feel involved in choosing their leaders and there are still ways available to influence major decisions made by those leaders once they are in power.

Dissent
Such a response makes more probable a breakdown of order. Dissent involves disagreement with the process by which leaders are chosen or impose themselves, and/or the objectives, the methods used or the final result of leadership decisions. However dissent by minority groups can be tolerated and contained in most societies, though this does depend upon the power of such groups. A small group of powerful military leaders can be sufficient to topple a civilian government – as for example in Bangladesh in 1975, where a group of officers toppled the civilian government of Sheikh Mujibar Rahman.

Nevertheless, the real threat to an established order is the way dissent by the majority is expressed.

The extent to which different countries can tolerate different types and levels of dissent depends upon historical factors and the type of political system which has emerged. Dissent can be expressed in a mild or extreme way. It may be articulated through the peaceful approaches of pressure groups trying to influence a government to accept or reject a certain course of action. A trade union may resort to strike action and public demonstrations to make known its dissent from a government decision. The most extreme and total expression of dissent, however, is revolution. An autocratic or dictatorial regime would view most expressions of public dissent as a threat to order and therefore place them in the category of civil disobedience. In liberal democracies, however, certain expressions of dissent are held to be a necessary and proper part of the democratic tradition. Within societies as heterogeneous as the liberal democracies, total agreement on any policy is impossible. In such societies it is essential for there to be adequate opportunity for dissent to be expressed in an acceptable manner. The uninhibited expression of public opinion, pressure group activity, peaceful demonstrations and official strike action are all accepted expressions of dissent in most liberal democracies. Violent dissent is generally unacceptable to all governments, for it brings with it a breakdown of social, political and economic order. Nevertheless, there are always exceptions. In 1966, for instance, Mao Tse-Tung fanned the flames of the Cultural Revolution among the Chinese masses in order to purge high-ranking opposition within his own government, and to strengthen his own position. The Cultural Revolution was a period of China's history during which many of the existing institutions within society disappeared in order to keep the Chinese Revolution 'pure'.

The reality is that, at any given time, in any particular country, the response of a populace to the policies of its leaders is a mixture of **compliance**, **consent** and **dissent**. The crucial question, in terms of political stability, is which of these responses is dominant?

Exercise
Which response is dominant in the UK?

The role of the law

Against this background it is possible to examine the role of **law** in the preservation of **order**.

The Oxford Dictionary gives this definition of law: 'a body of enacted or customary rules recognized by a community as binding'.

Laws follow logically from the high value placed upon order by human beings living within communities. Without laws there would be no basis for living together peacefully, no basis for ordered progress. It is useful here to remind ourselves of the role of a constitution. It is a set of first principles by which a society decides to be guided. These principles deal with what governmental functions need to be fulfilled, who should fulfil them, the limits to their power and authority and what basic rights a citizen should be given. All statute laws, in the UK for example, are enacted by the constitutionally *created* legitimate authority, parliament.

The **law** can be seen to have a dual role: first, it enables those who govern to maintain control and to make changes which they consider to be beneficial, and second, it protects the rights of citizens individually and in groups by setting out the legal relationships between citizen(s) and citizen(s), and citizen(s) and government. Emphasis upon one or other aspect of the role of law varies within the historical experience of a particular country and from one country to another. Law-making in some countries is the prerogative of a governing class who make laws in their own interests and disregard the rest of the population. This was the case in Britain until the Great Reform Act of 1832. A liberal democracy strives to achieve a balance between the need of a government to maintain control while applying a programme of change and provision for the protection of the constitutionally stated rights of all citizens. It is important here to make a distinction between *laws* and *conventions*. Conventions are informal rules which arise during the development of any political system. They are patterns of behaviour tried and tested over time thus providing acceptable ways of achieving objectives. They are the 'oil' which keeps the political machine lubricated. Unlike a law the breaking of a convention does not entail a legal penalty, though there may be social or political penalties involved. There are many official positions and institutions which are the creation of convention, including the British premiership and the cabinet.

Discussion point

Some people, notably anarchists, feel that law places unnecessary barriers between individuals and that laws should be abolished. Would such a course lead to a more co-operative, less selfish society, as anarchists claim, or to chaos? Would you act differently if there were no laws to control you?

Justice

It is important from the outset to distinguish the features of the concept of justice. The exercise of fairness and impartiality in devising laws and the application of these same criteria in applying those laws are both features of a just system. In Britain such ideas of **justice** are taken into account by those who make laws and those who interpret them. The *rule of law* is a principle of the British Constitution which is intended to provide a just legal system. Inherent in this concept is the idea not only that every citizen shall be equally bound by open, fair laws enforced by impartial judges, but also that the relationship between the government and every individual shall be controlled in the same way as those of individuals with each other. Only in this way can the rights of the individual be protected and asserted against governmental abuse of power. (Refer back to the discussion of this point in Chapter 2.)

Yet laws themselves may be unjust. They may be devised by a dictator to preserve his own power by subjugating a population or by one group to dominate others, even in liberal democracies. Nevertheless whatever its source, to be found guilty of breaking the law automatically brings punishment. The knowledge of punishment for law-breaking is a sufficient deterrent to keep most people law-abiding most of the time.

In many democratic societies the legal code follows closely ideas prevalent in those societies of the nature of right and wrong. Such ideas are often rooted in religion, traditions and customs, and individuals come to accept them as part of their own system of values. Therefore, in addition to laws acting as a deterrent, individual conscience acts as a control mechanism.

Is there ever a case for breaking the law?

At an individual level it is generally held that action in self-defence is acceptable. In a wider context this question needs to be related to dissident groups within society. It has already been established that in the interests of stability through ordered change, the laws must be observed by all. Nevertheless it is noteworthy that rebellious expression is a feature of the British experience. Intensity of feeling in pursuit of a cause does, on occasion, well up into unlawful actions. The history of the British Labour Movement and the Suffragette Movement is rich with examples.

Is there ever a case for breaking the law in order to overthrow a government?

This is a most complex question, to which only the groundwork of an answer can be provided here. For those in government, such a violent challenge would be an act of rebellion by terrorists. Yet those in the rebellious group would see themselves as freedom fighters, believing right to be on their side. Such are the beliefs of:

(a) The mujaheddin ('holy warrior') guerrillas fighting the Soviet-backed Afghanistan government
(b) The US-backed Contras fighting the left-wing Sandanista government of Nicaragua
(c) The Basque separatists fighting the Spanish government
(d) The Eritrean guerrillas* fighting the Ethiopian government
(e) The IRA fighting the British government
(f) The black African National Congress (ANC) opposition to the white minority South African government.

Although it is beyond the scope of this book to analyse the rights and wrongs of the conflicts cited, it would be useful to consider them briefly against the ideas of the British philosopher John Locke (1632–1704). According to his notion of the *Social Contract*, the authority of a government rests upon a bargain with the people. Citizens agree to give certain powers to the government and obey its laws, while the

---

*EPLF (Eritrean People's Liberation Front); TPLF (Tigre People's Liberation Front)

government is obliged to exercise such powers in the interests of all. Locke established the political sovereignty of the people, and therefore their ultimate right to overthrow a government which abused its power. It is ironical, though hardly surprising, that the theory of the Social Contract provided American colonists with the moral justification for rebellion against British rule under George III in 1776.

Where the gap between the government and the people is such that leaders have no means of knowing, let alone trying to fulfil, the wishes of the people, there is a strong possibility that underground movements will form and resort to violent methods to challenge the existing government. At this stage the outcome depends upon the numbers involved on each side, plus military skills and weaponry.

A further factor is the level of external support for the incumbent government and/or the rebellious group. The military rebels who overthrew President Allende of Chile in 1973 would have had greater difficulty in gaining power had it not been for the covert support of the US Central Intelligence Agency (CIA). Such a situation is not isolated – throughout history many such cases have occurred. In some nation-states oppression is so absolute that this sequence of events seems highly probable. However, the social, economic and political destructiveness of such conflict is clear, and therefore many countries have evolved democratic mechanisms to forestall such developments.

In 1986 events in South Africa were moving rapidly to a climax. It would be a useful exercise to review the discussion point below as a black South African and/or a white South African. Use your knowledge of the situation in that country, and bear in mind the analytical points raised above.

Discussion point
Under what circumstances would you consider breaking the law? How would you justify your actions?

The British experience

The British political system has evolved over centuries and has become the model for many liberal–democratic states which have emerged more recently. Governmental power has gradually shifted from a near-absolute monarchy ruling with a parliament dominated by a small class of landed aristocrats, to a group of representatives elected by the people. This change to some extent explains how Britain has evolved a system which achieves a high degree of political stability and order. It has been established that a nation's survival and progress depends upon a government gaining the consent, or at least the compliance, of a majority of citizens for its policies. This has been achieved by the oppression of dictators and oligarchies in totalitarian societies but in liberal democracies, Britain included, it is the development of democratic institutions which has made possible the gaining of majority consent by the leadership.

The basic principle which underlies the present political structure in Britain is the belief that all adults should have the opportunity to shape their own destiny. To this purpose universal adult suffrage has been established, pressure groups are free to lobby the government to further their interests and people are free to express their views publicly through the mass media. There is a much greater chance that a government will gain the consent of the people for their policies if it has been elected by them and if there are channels for consultation before courses of action are devised and implemented. Where these basic democratic mechanisms are absent there is a greater possibility of law-breaking and disorder. Political parties, therefore, seek a consensus, they seek to formulate a set of policies which will gain the support of a majority of electors. The electors themselves are presented with a variety of programmes for change from which to select.

At a more fundamental level a consensus operates based upon accepted procedures for change. Certain kinds of dissent are accepted and contained within the institutional framework, for example, demonstrations and strikes. In this way the chances of more extreme expressions of disorder, such as riots or rebellion, are lessened. This consensus on the chosen pattern of ordered change is contained in the constitution.

At each election the majority of voters endorse the accepted procedure for choosing representatives through their participation by voting. This in turn provides a degree of **legitimacy** for the government to maintain order according to the law.

Dissent is usually within the law if it is peaceful. For example, the hard won fight of trade unionists to picket is only lawful if it is peaceful picketing. In the same way street parades are only lawful if they do not threaten the peace.

The law in Britain is applied by the judicial arm of government. The independence of the judiciary is preserved according to the doctrine of the separation of powers. If this doctrine were observed to the letter then the functions of each of the major arms of government – legislative, executive, judiciary – would be exercised by different officials, to avoid the concentration of power to the point of tyranny. This doctrine is only partially operated within the British political system – at certain points there is more a fusion of powers than a separation. The monarch and the Lord Chancellor provide two examples of this fusion, but more importantly the cabinet includes those who control the legislature and head the executive. A fair distance, however, is still retained between the judiciary and the other two arms of government, for only if this were so could there be a credible application of the rule of law.

It is clear that without laws there could be no society. In ancient Britain, as with many other societies, the rules of society were those of custom and taboo. The war-lord king interpreted the law, dispensed penalties and provided protection for his subjects. As society became more complex so did the rules of society. They become formally codified into written laws and a judicial system was created to adjudicate in disputes and pass judgment on those who were found to have broken the laws.

The laws applied in Britain may be divided into criminal and civil. *Criminal law* identifies offences against society or the individual, which are punishable, usually by imprisonment or a fine. Examples include murder and theft. The main point here is to punish someone for contravening society's rules and deterring others from doing so. *Civil law* identifies disputes between individuals or groups, such as divorce or a claim by a factory worker for an industrial injury. The main point here is the settling of a dispute.

Both criminal and civil laws are man-made but they may rest on more fundamental divine and natural laws. *Divine law* is that revealed by God to man. The Ten Commandments revealed to Moses are laws of this kind. Some may be included within the body of a state's criminal law, others may not. The commandment 'Thou shalt not kill' has become the centre of a British criminal law, but the commandment 'Thou shalt love the Lord thy God with all thy heart and with all thy mind and thou shalt have no other gods but me', has not. An interesting development in Iran, since the exile of the Shah, has been the rigid and often harsh application of divine law as interpreted by the Islamic leaders – for example, the withdrawal of freedoms given to women under the previous regime and their return to a traditional subservient role.

Natural law rests on what men believe to be their inalienable rights, that is, those entitlements which are part of being human. There is no universal agreement about natural rights, a fact which is well illustrated by the way that philosophers have written and argued about them for centuries. Nevertheless, many written constitutions contain a Bill of Rights which sets out the entitlements of citizenship in a particular country. The first ten amendments to the US Consitution comprise their Bill of Rights. Contravention of these constitutional provisions is punishable in American courts of law. English courts also try to observe rules of natural justice, for example, that no man should act as a judge in a case in which he is in any way involved.

Man-made law (criminal and civil) is derived from *common law*, which is based on custom and precedent developed through the centuries, statute law (Acts of Parliament) and equity (a body of legal doctrine which covers weaknesses in the common law). A useful guide to what is the law is that which the courts interpret as such.

The legal personnel who interpret the law in Britain includes judges, barristers and solicitors. Judges of the High Court are appointed by the Queen on the advice of the Prime Minister and the Lord Chancellor. The Lords of Appeal in Ordinary, the Lord Chief Justice and the Master of the Rolls are nominated by the Prime Minister. Since the Act of Settlement in 1701, judges can only be removed from office as a result of an Address (or request) to the Monarch passed by both Houses of Parliament. Their salaries are paid directly from the Consolidated Fund (the government's bank account). At the other end of the scale magistrates preside over Petty

Sessional Courts, these are appointed by the Lord Chancellor.

The Lord Chancellor himself, as with other members of the Cabinet, is chosen by the Prime Minister. His position is both political and judicial. Politically his function is to advise the government on legal matters, but as a judge convention requires that he acts impartially.

The British legal profession also includes barristers, who may appear in any court and solicitors (advocates), who may only appear in magistrates courts and county courts. Anyone who seeks legal advice or representation first approaches a solicitor who may in turn take advice from a barrister or engage him to represent his client in court. In this way solicitors keep in daily touch with their client while barristers preserve a degree of detachment.

It would be inadequate appraisal if this presentation of the British judiciary were left untouched. The theoretical impartiality of the judiciary has been analysed in depth by J. A. G. Griffith in his book *The Politics of the Judiciary*. According to Griffith:

> there is something of a dilemma in the judiciary's position as both upholders of law and order and protectors of the individual against a powerful Executive. ... In these terms, the judiciary may come into conflict with the Government of the day ... where [it] acts 'illegally'. ... Thus they set limits to the discretionary powers of Governments and to the rights of individuals especially where these two forces conflict.

Griffith analyses the view of impartiality as being based upon judicial neutrality. This he holds to be a myth.

> In denying such neutrality, I am not concerned merely to argue that judges, like other people, have their own personal political convictions. ... What matters is the function they perform and the role they perceive themselves as fulfilling in the political structure. Neither impartiality nor independence necessarily involves neutrality. Judges are part of the machinery of authority within the State and as such cannot avoid making political decisions.

While Griffith concludes that judges endeavour to act in the public interest he believes that they have a special view of what the public interest is. He cites the oligarchic nature of political power in Britain, in other words that power is concentrated in the hands of a few people, and includes senior judges amongst this small group of politically powerful people.

The importance of their task, their influence on behaviour, the extent of their powers, the status they enjoy confirm beyond question their place within the governing group. And, like other members of the group, they show themselves alert to protect the social order from threats to its stability or to the existing distribution of political and economic power.

Developments in the 1980s indicate that those in authority place an even higher priority on the preservation of social order than before. It is arguable that events have pushed governments into adopting a firmer line. The intractable problems of Northern Ireland, the violence associated with the bitter miners' strike of 1984–5, soccer violence, inner-city clashes in Toxteth, Liverpool (July 1981), Brixton, London (1981 and September 1985), Handsworth, Birmingham (September 1985) and the Broadwater Farm Estate, Tottenham, London (October 1985) – provide a catalogue of disturbances with which government has had to contend. Many attempts have been made to analyse the causes of disorder. Some point to the disintegration of family life and lack of discipline in schools. Others single out the frustration and despair of disadvantaged groups such as inner-city black youths and the unemployed. Whatever the reasons, the response of government has been to increase police numbers and powers to counter disorder.

The Public Order Bill before parliament in 1986 illustrates this trend. The new Act will affect marches, assemblies and pickets. It will give the senior officer present the power to impose any conditions or give any directions on a march, the right to decide on the place at which a protest may be held, the maximum number of people who can attend, and the length of time they may protest. Failure to comply will involve three months' imprisonment or a £1000 fine for the organizers. In addition to extra powers being given to the police, old offences such as riot and affray are redefined more strictly, and new offences such as violent disorder are created.

According to the Public Order Bill 1986, the definition of the offence of riot is as follows:

Where twelve or more persons who are present together use or

threaten unlawful violence for a common purpose and the conduct of
them (taken together) is such as would cause a person of reasonable
firmness present at the scene to fear for his personal safety, each of
the persons is guilty of riot.

The maximum sentence is life imprisonment, a fine, or both.

Exercise

There are those in society who see this Bill as a threat to
individual and group rights: a relentless movement towards an
intrusive police state. Others regard it as a necessary response
to ensure the protection of law-abiding citizens and the
stability of the state. What is your assessment?

The guardians of law and order

The police

All major societies require some degree of policing to cope
with the protection of life and property, the preservation of
law and order and the apprehending of offenders. In many
countries, however, the police become the agents of oppressive rulers and as such are feared by the population. A more
sinister type of policing is sometimes performed by a secret
police force which often employs covert tactics in the course of
their work. Such undercover work provides fertile ground for
those who write thrillers for the bookstand, television or the
cinema. Perhaps the most notorious secret police force was
that of the Third Reich in Germany – the Gestapo. By the
nature of their work secret police forces adopt behaviour
which is on the verges of what is legally acceptable, and in
many cases seem to go beyond their legitimate tasks. The
Central Intelligence Agency (CIA) has suffered badly from
disclosures about some of their activities which have been
illegal. In Britain there is little apparent democratic control
over the actions of whatever security forces exist, and the
nature of the security forces is kept a well-guarded secret. Two
opposing descriptions of the security services in Britain may
be found in Chapman Pincher, *Inside Story*, and Tony Bunyon,
The Political Police in Britain.

The British police forces, however, have developed as
essentially civilian, unarmed bodies. Their task is to preserve
order and protect the lives and property of British citizens.

The policeman is an instrument of the law, seeking primarily to secure the observance of the law. Over the past decade there has been an increasing willingness on the part of senior policemen to involve themselves more in political debate as to the role of the police and Griffith's doubts about the neutrality of judges also may be applicable in the case of the police force. Some groups, particularly those on the left and many organizations representing coloured people, in Britain would argue that the police are increasingly involved as agents of government policy. The use of the police to intervene in industrial disputes and to protect certain political groups, such as the National Front, are often seen as examples of this. Equally, the way in which the police may use their discretion to prosecute certain groups can be seen as a political decision on their part. The 'sus' laws have now been repealed because of the feeling that they were being used in a discriminatory fashion by some members of the police. There remains a strong feeling, particularly among ethnic minorities, that some policemen do not treat all people equally and that certain groups are singled out by the police.

The escalation of violent clashes between disenchanted groups and the police in the 1980s has brought about more militaristic styles of policing. Legislation which intends to expand police powers has already been noted in the last section. In addition, the equipment available to police is now much more formidable – CS gas, plastic bullets and longer truncheons. Riot shields, visored helmets and armoured cars also reflect the protective needs of the police in violent situations. The thinking behind such changes is indicated in this comment by Sir Kenneth Newman, the Metropolitan Police Chief, reported in the *Financial Times* (23 March 1983):

It would be better if we stopped talking about crime prevention and lifted the whole thing to a higher level of generality represented by the words 'social control'.

There is a body of opinion which holds that, while a hard line adopted by the police effectively quells violent outbursts, it also creates bitter resentment and therefore a potentiality for further disorder. Moreover, the police are increasingly seen as state agents for social control rather than crime prevention, in Northern Ireland and flash-point inner-city areas. The

Runnymede Trust reported in 1986 that since the October 1985 clashes in Tottenham, 350 arrests had been made on the Broadwater Farm Estate and 120 people had been charged, mainly black youths. It appears that high-crime groups and areas are identified, rather like the criminal rookeries of Dickensian London.

A further dimension of disquiet derives from the suspicion of intelligence-gathering methods through community policing. Surveillance of perceived potential 'subversives', whether individuals or groups, is a more apparent police tactic. On one hand powerful arguments are advocated in support of such measures, while on the other fears are expressed that basic democratic freedoms and rights are under threat. Those of the latter view believe that the tradition of democratic challenge to the accepted policies of the time is being seriously curtailed. One aspect of British democracy is to express views freely – even if they are, at the time, unpalatable to many in society. The history of the Labour Movement and the Suffragettes bears witness to this sometimes painful dynamic of constructive change.

Discussion point

Is there a danger that in the legitimate pursuit of order by government agencies, there can be a tendency to 'criminalize' too many activities in society?

Before considering this question read the following quotation made by a former Chief Constable, Mr Harold Salisbury, in 1981. A definition of a subversive:

Anyone who shows affinity towards Communism, that's common sense, the IRA, the PLO, and I would say anyone who's decrying marriage, family life, trying to break that up, pushing drugs, homosexuality, indiscipline in schools, weak penalties for anti-social crimes.

A whole gamut of things like that, that could be pecking away at the foundations of our society and weakening it.

The military

If rebellious groups in a society were to create such a disturbance that the police were unable to cope then the armed forces would be called in to restore law and order. The military is always a power to be reckoned with in supporting the police during times of internal disturbance. Nowhere is this more graphically evidenced than in Northern Ireland, where the Royal Ulster Constabulary reinforced by the British Army has tried to maintain order in a province torn by sectarian violence. This apart, however, the usual role of the military is to repel external aggression by another country.

In Western democracies such as Great Britain and the USA, as in stable communist countries such as the USSR, the military fulfils its traditional roles as set out above. This is possible where there is a legitimate, strong civilian government operating with reasonable success. Field Marshal Lord Carver, in a BBC interview with Desmond Wilcox, commented that he opposed political involvement by military personnel and added his belief that one of the main protections against the involvement of the army in the internal affairs of Britain is a free press and a free news media. It is reasonable to express such a view within a stable British context but it is something of a luxury within the context of many countries, particularly those in the Third World but also including in the recent past Western European countries such as Spain, Portugal and Greece. Military leaders in many countries have seized, or have felt obliged to be drawn into, political leadership. The entry of the military into politics is usually related to major political, economic and social changes. For example in some countries, after the transition from colony to independent nation, military leaders have been obliged to preserve the ideals of the independence movement, where corrupt and divided political groups have created confusion. The military claims that with its emphasis upon discipline and efficiency, it is able to take the reins of government and settle affairs for the good of all.

A detailed analysis of political involvement by military groups need not detain us beyond a brief review of three main types of intervention, all of which are related to weaknesses in civilian leadership.

The military may act directly as the force for reform or revolution. In the Philippines the support of the armed forces for Mrs Aquino was the decisive factor which led to the overthrow of President Marcos. It became clear that the corrupt regime of Marcos had lost the support of the military; when this happened he found it impossible to remain in power.

Another form of involvement takes place when military

leaders form a 'caretaker' government to restore order where civilian government has broken down. Burma provides a good illustration of this kind of intervention. General Ne Win twice took governmental control from Prime Minister U Nu in 1958 and 1962 to save Burma from civil war after disastrous experiments in democracy. Eventually Ne Win civilianized* his government and has remained in power to this day. Turkey also has seen military interventions of the 'caretaker' type. It is, however, also a fact that military leaders are often reluctant to return control to civilians after tasting governmental power.

A third type of military involvement is as the 'backer' of a civilian government, that is, the civilian government depends upon the support of the military in order to stay in power. Such a situation is not uncommon in the Third World. For twenty years prior to 1965 the military supported the government of President Sukarno in Indonesia. After 1965 the military gradually took control and Sukarno was finally replaced by the government of General Suharto. The military-backed government of the Shah of Iran crumbled in the face of a fundamental Islamic revival led by the Ayatollah Khomeini. More recently, the withdrawal of US backing for the regime of President Ferdinand Marcos of the Philippines made possible a switch of support by the Filipino military, led by Lt General Ramos, to Mrs Corazon Aquino who became the new president in February 1986 after a bloodless revolution. In the same month, President Jean-Claude ('Baby Doc') Duvalier of Haiti fled the country for France. His regime toppled after the US government and the local military withdrew support. The Duvalier dynasty ('Papa Doc' Duvalier 1957–71, and 'Baby Doc' Duvalier 1971–86) was marked by corruption and repression. Gross economic mismanagement, coupled with the atrocities wrought by the Tontons Macoutes, the Duvalier private army, finally brought about the fall of the government and its replacement by a civilian–military council in February 1986.

---

* Ne Win and his officers relinquished their military titles in order to be more acceptable to the Burmese people. It was decided a more permanent government could secure more legitimacy if its officials were civilians rather than military men. Since then the government has implemented far-reaching reforms under the banner of 'The Burmese way to socialism'.

Conclusion

Order is the most fundamental of political concepts for without it there would be no organized communities which we could recognize as societies. Only those seeking the breakdown of society for their own political ends, for example, anarchists, would wish for continued disorder. Indeed, history reveals how men prefer to live under an oppressive kind of order rather than have no order at all. Such evidence indicates the basic need of man to know where he stands. This says nothing, however, of what is the best kind of order. It is this quest which is the subject of constant debate. When the media report statistics illustrating rising crime rates or street clashes between rival groups, people are quick to deplore what they interpret as a breakdown in law and order. But, such comments are based upon an evaluation of how much the existing state of affairs falls short of their ideal perception of order. In Western democratic societies, it is believed that lasting stability and order is closely related to key ideas which take identifiable form in the political life of a nation. Adherence to constitutional principles has already been examined, it is now necessary to shed further light by exploring the concepts of power, authority, representation and responsibility.

Essay questions

1   'If the public are to be protected by the police, they must also be protected from the police.' Discuss. (Oxford, Summer 1981)
2   'In a democracy and in a dictatorship the reasons why people obey the law are the same; the reasons why they should obey the law are quite different.' Discuss. (Oxford, Summer 1981)
3   Is terrorism ever justified? (Oxford, Summer 1982)
4   Are the police too powerful? (Oxford, Summer 1983)
    Read Chapter 4 before attempting this question.
5   What is meant by saying that government should rest on the 'consent of the governed'? (Oxford, Summer 1984)
6   What is 'the rule of law' and what is necessary to safeguard it? (Oxford, Summer 1984)
7   'The police should be the servants of the community:

in practice they are a law unto themselves.' Discuss.
(Oxford, Summer 1985)

8   Why should policing have become such a contentious
issue in British politics in the last ten years? (Cambridge,
Summer 1984)

9   What are the limits in Britain to political toleration, and
what should they be? (London, January 1981)

10 What is the rôle of the police in maintaining public order?
Are there legitimate criticisms of how they fulfil this rôle?
(London, June 1981)

11 When should the citizen defy the state? (London,
January 1982)

12 'The police, because of their justified concern with
public order, are bound to act repressively.' Discuss.
(London, June 1982)

13 What forms of protest against government do you
consider legitimate, and what forms illegitimate?
(London, June 1984)

14 How tolerant should the authorities be towards threats of
violence against the state or social groups? (London,
January 1986)

15 'Neither politicians nor pressure groups nor anyone else
may tell the police what decisions to take, or what
methods to employ, or whether or not to enforce the law
in a particular case' (Lord Scarman). Discuss this view of
police accountability. (London, January 1986)

16 Can there be any justification for recent outbreaks of
violence in the United Kingdom? (London, June 1986)

17 Describe and account for the developments in extra-
parliamentary forms of protest since the 1960s. (AEB
Specimen Question 1986)

Short-answer questions

1   Define the concept of public order. (London, January
1981)

2   What is meant by 'the rule of law'? (London, January 1985)

3   Define the concept of 'government by consent'. (London,
June 1985)

4   List the main characteristics of the rule of law. (London,
June 1985)

5   What is meant by equality before the law? (London, June
1986)

4 Power and authority

Power is the ability to get things done, to make others do what you want – even if they do not want to do it. A variety of means can be used to persuade people to do things, but power always has as its base the ability to reward or punish.

From this outline it becomes clear that power is not something that only exists at a national or international level; power exists wherever people are involved in relationships – at a family level, in school, in work or even when playing sports. Within the family parents have considerable power over their children, they can make them eat cabbage, go to bed or wash behind their ears. When children are older they may have a strict time by which they should be home. Children do as they are told, to a large extent, because their parents can back up their instructions with either rewards or punishments, including the ultimate expression of power – *force*. Within certain limits parents may use force to discipline children and most children are aware of this – but force is not used very often, the threat of it is enough.

Many children realize that their parents can control them. Some also realize that they have some power over their parents. Again this power is based on *rewards* and *punishments*. Children can also, to some extent, punish parents – through tantrums, lack of co-operation and so on. Usually, though, parents have more power than children – and so can win any struggle. Yet this illustrates a major point. We all have some power – the problem is one of degree: who has more power than me and who has most power of all?

To analyse any power relationship it is necessary to look at who has some power, not at who does not have any.

Discussion point

Try to analyse your school or college – who has power over you, what rewards or punishment can they inflict on you? Who has power over your teacher, whom do you have power over? Discuss your analysis with the rest of your group.

Children do not only obey their parents because they know that their parents can reward or punish them, they also believe that their parents have a right, based on age, experience or simply because they are parents, to be able to tell them what to do (even if they may not always like it). At school, teachers are not simply obeyed because of their power – pupils accept that teachers should be in a position to tell them what to do. In the main individuals accept that the government should be in a position to run the country.

There are considerable disadvantages for a government which depends solely upon military power to maintain control. In the long term it is important for all people in positions of power that they should have their position recognized as legitimate (rightful) by those over whom they have power. Professor Crick, in his article, 'Basic concepts for political education', has this to say:

Probably all government requires some capacity for or potentiality of force or violence; but probably no government can maintain itself through time, as distinct from defence and attack at specific moments, without legitimating itself in some way, getting itself loved, respected, even just accepted as inevitable, otherwise it would need constant recourse to open violence – which is rarely the case.

Authority is the quality of being able to get people to do things because they think the individual or group has the right to tell them what to do. Those in authority are followed because it is believed that they fulfil a need within the community or political system. Authority, then, is linked to respect, which creates **legitimacy** and, therefore, leads to power.

A distinction needs to be made here between authority and authoritarian. All governments need authority for people to accept their right to make decisions. Not all governments are authoritarian. Authoritarian regimes are those which rely heavily on coercion, on making people do what the governments want, irrespective of their wishes. This is often done by the use of arbitrary imprisonment, use of the armed forces and secret police. A more commonplace example may make this clear: a teacher can control a class in a number of ways, often by his authority as an expert. Some teachers rely instead on the exercise of strict controls, punishments and limited freedom of action for individuals – such behaviour can be seen as authoritarian. Because such a situation can be unpleasant for the individuals concerned there is an automatic tendency to criticize such an approach, yet it may have its advantages at times and may, in some circumstances, be necessary. A teacher with an unruly class last thing on a Friday afternoon may have to be authoritarian in order to get any work done.

Discussion point
Is there any time, in a democratic society when there is a need for authoritarian action? How can we ensure that such action can be controlled?

Perhaps an example might clarify this. In the past in Britain the church had great secular as well as spiritual power – it was a large landowner, it had its own courts and it could control to some extent the lives of ordinary people. In the twentieth century the control of the church over people's lives has declined – fewer people attended services and many churches have closed. Successive governments have taken over many of the functions previously carried out by the church, for example, in areas such as education and health care. Even so the church and church leaders still have considerable authority. The intervention of the Archbishop of Canterbury's special envoy, Mr Terry Waite, into many potentially explosive situations and his ability to produce results is indicative of the great authority still exercized by the church. Mr Waite, in Iran in 1981 and Libya in 1985, was responsible for securing the release of detainees being held hostage when conventional methods had failed.

According to the German writer Max Weber (1864–1920), there are three main types of authority: traditional, legal–rational and charismatic.

Traditional authority is legitimated by appealing to the past. It often looks back to old customs and the acts of ancestors. Weber claims this is the type of authority typical of simpler, pre-industrial societies.

Legal–rational authority is legitimated by appealing to rules and laws. The British government has authority because it was elected by a legal process and because it works within the laws of the land. This type of authority is typical of industrial countries.

Charismatic authority is based on the personal attributes of an individual which give him the ability to get others to follow, even if they have to break the law. Hitler and Mussolini could be examples of charismatic leaders, as could Jesus. Charisma is very rare and societies with charismatic leaders often have difficulties in replacing them.

These are ideal types of authority and are unlikely to exist in their pure form. Britain, for instance, has a government based largely on legal–rational authority, but with some element of tradition (for example, the monarchy) and from time to time some elements of charismatic leadership (for example, Churchill).

Exercise

What is the difference between power and authority?
   Give one example of:
(a)   a person or group with a lot of power but little authority
(b)   a person or group with a lot of authority but little power

Types of power

We have already seen that power can exist at an almost infinite number of levels but we will now have to concentrate upon an analysis of different types of power at a national level. Here it becomes necessary to try to distinguish between different types of power, for individuals may be very powerful in some fields but not in others – although we will see later there is a considerable overlap. These divisions of power can be seen as a consequence of a type of society in which there is considerable division of functions – a complex society will develop certain complex and specialized groups to deal with particular types of problems. Their expertise will give them power over the non-expert majority, often linked with the ability to make life pleasant or unpleasant for the mass of

people. We can identify three main concentrations of power in modern Britain:
(*a*)   political power
(*b*)   economic power
(*c*)   military power

Political power
For the purposes of this discussion we shall take the concept of politics as being concerned with those decisions which affect the way a society is organized and the goals which that society chooses to pursue. Conflict about goals and ways of achieving them is an inevitable feature of such a definition.

In Britain it is the party which gains a majority of MPs in the House of Commons which forms a government. The leader of that party usually becomes Prime Minister and together with his or her chosen cabinet formulates policies which are then passed to parliament for discussion. A government with a working majority can usually get its way.

At one level, then, political power rests with the government (some would go further and say that it rests increasingly with the Prime Minister), but if parliament has supreme legislative power – it is sovereign – then *it* must be the repository of political power. As we have seen, parliament has limitations to this sovereignty but it can still exert strong political control, even to the extent of causing a government to resign and forcing a general election, as experienced by the minority Labour Government in early 1979. A minority government is particularly vulnerable to such pressure but even a majority government could be under threat from a major revolt of its own back-benches.

Within parliament there has traditionally been a struggle for pre-eminence between the House of Lords and the House of Commons. This has led to the House of Lords losing many, but not all, of its powers. The House of Lords can show its teeth from time to time even if it is only to block bills. The Labour Party would claim that the House of Lords with its inbuilt conservative bias tends only to show its teeth when there is a Labour government as in the case of the attempted blocking of the Trade Union and Labour Relations (Amendment) Bill of 1975.

Even if a party does not form the government under the British parliamentary system it can retain a certain amount of

power. Her Majesty's Opposition to some people seems to be
a negative institution – blind opposition for the sake of it.
This is a mistaken view for the Opposition serves to keep
the government of the day on its toes, provide an alternative
government for the electorate to choose if the occasion should
arise, and attempts to amend what it considers to be
misguided, excessive or ill-considered government legislation.
In times of minority government, for example, the 1974–9
Labour Government, opposition parties can limit the activities
of government. The Liberal Party would claim that during the
Lib-Lab Pact of 1977–8 it stopped the Labour Party from
pursuing socialist policies, and persuaded the government to
adopt some Liberal policies, a clear exercise of political power.

Party, parliament and government hold much political
power in Britain but, many would argue, it is the individual
who has supreme power. The major difficulty is that many
others would argue persuasively that the individual has little
or *no* power. The act of voting can be seen as an expression of
the will of the people – democracy is, after all, 'people power',
but the extent to which an individual can influence the
outcome of an election is minimal. His ability to influence
political events between elections may be less, but he can try.
Just as the individual voter often feels powerless, so, too, do
many back-bench MPs who feel themselves to be controlled
by the party machine which 'whips' them into line. MPs are
able to ask questions, designed to reveal the shortcomings
of a government and to introduce Private Members' Bills.
However, the need for specialists in government and the cloak
of Whitehall secrecy which still falls over much government
business has led back-benchers to feel that they lack real power.

The position is somewhat complicated by the narrow
definition of 'political power' so far adopted, for we have seen
in recent years that power may be leaving the hands of other
powerful bodies. With the downfall of two governments; the
Conservative Government 1970–4 and the Labour Government 1974–9, there has been increasing speculation that other
centres of power are becoming concerned in politics – the
main brunt of the attack has been aimed at trades unions.
There seems to be much doubt as to how far it is now possible
to talk of political power as being divorced from other types of
power. The relationship between these various 'political' and

'non-political' elements and which is likely to be most dominant, is discussed further in a later part of this chapter.

Economic power

The wealth of a nation depends on the extent to which it can produce goods and services efficiently and the way that those with economic power help or hinder such production. In the twentieth century governments have become increasingly involved in regulating economic forces by introducing price controls, trades' union legislation, import restrictions and taking control of large sectors of manufacturing and service industry, including steel production and the railway service. The fact that government is now a major employer serves to underline the difficulties involved in separating economic and political power. Despite this there are three main groups which can wield considerable economic power apart from the government. These are:

1 industrial combines (including multi-national companies operating in Britain, such as Unilever)
2 trades unions
3 financial institutions

Before proceeding to a further examination of these, it is worth noting that there are numerous external organizations which from time to time exert economic pressures on British governments, from beyond our national boundaries. The impact of such organizations has been mentioned in the context of the limitations to parliamentary sovereignty in Chapter 2, but when considering the internal economic situation it is worth remembering the constraints upon governments imposed by such organizations as the International Monetary Fund, the European Economic Community and the Organization of Petroleum Exporting Countries.

Industrial combines

Through their control of employment and production and their central position in the wealth creation process, industrialists are able to wield great power. Most of the wealth producing sector of the economy (mainly the privately owned sector) has as its main aim the making of profit. If industrialists do not feel that there is sufficient prospect for reasonable profits they can exercise their judgement and limit investment and employment. On these sort of commercial decisions the well-being of the nation depends. If, on the other hand, there are good prospects for profit and efficiency then the nation benefits from having more goods and higher employment coupled perhaps with rising living standards.

This type of argument is often put forward by groups such as the Confederation of British Industry to explain why industrialists are such a vital sector of the community that they should receive as much encouragement as possible with as few restraints as possible. This view of industrialists as working in the 'national interest' has led some politicians, often Conservative, to argue that the growth of trades union power has so reduced the ability of British industry to retain a competitive edge in international markets, that the result has been frustration and a dilution of incentive among industrialists. They go on to argue that it is necessary to stem the growth of trades union power in order to release the productive forces of the economy. This view stresses the way in which industrialists benefit the whole nation while trades unions act just for a sector of the community.

Exercise
What are the implications of equating the activities of industrialists with the 'national interest', and those of trades unions with 'sectional interest', or *vice versa*?

Although the above argument presents industrialists in a favourable light it is questionable whether they always act in the national interest or even whether it is their primary intention to do so. Many companies are now multi-nationals whose interests extend over much of the world, and are not linked with the well-being of one country, but with the firm. Multi-nationals are now in a position where many smaller countries, and from time to time, larger countries, are almost powerless to hinder their activities. A more wide-ranging criticism has come from people like Professor R. Miliband who has argued that the controllers of industry are able to exert permanent pressure on government because of their power to make decisions which will affect the way the economy expands. According to Miliband, trades unions often seem to have more power because their dealings with government, and hence their successes, are more public. Industrialists, he argues, have more power, and this is strengthened by their social and economic backgrounds, which tend to be similar to those of politicians and top civil servants. It seems likely, then, that politicians may be more 'in tune' with the ideas of industry than of labour.

Trades unions

Trades unions seek to represent, and improve the conditions of workers. They grew up to represent mainly manual workers and this is still where their main strength lies, for example, the Transport and General Workers Union, at present with about 1.5 million members, is the biggest union in Britain. Increasingly, non-manual workers are joining trades unions such as the Association of Scientific, Technical and Managerial Staff and the National Association of Local Government Officers. Out of a work-force of about 26.5 million in 1984–5, about 9.85 million were members of trades unions affiliated to the TUC.

Trades unions gain their power from their high membership. An old trades union slogan is 'Unity is strength' and this reflects union attitudes. An individual worker has little power or influence but when he joins a union he and his colleagues can have great power. This visible type of power that unions have tends to be of a negative sort. They can disrupt industry by taking various kinds of action, the most extreme kind of which is the strike. This ability to disrupt not only affects the industry concerned, but also the general public. Impact may be immediate – for example, the dock strikes in 1984 – or cumulative, such as the miners' strike from March 1984 to March 1985. The violence associated with picketing during the miners' strike not only incensed many members of the public, but also caused tension between the leadership of the TUC and the Labour Party on the one hand, and militant elements of the NUM on the other. This was brought to the fore when Mr Norman Willis, General Secretary of the TUC, expressed the organization's condemnation of all violence 'from whatever quarter it comes', in November 1985.

However, there is a positive side to union power which operates unobtrusively to keep the economic system functioning. Unions prevent many worker problems reaching a serious level through their routine work; yet such work receives little publicity. Employers recognize, from a practical point of view, the value of continuing consultation with a single committee of workers' representatives, and some favour the closed shop for this reason. Under such an arrangement a worker would not be accepted for employment unless he belonged to a relevant union. The right of an individual to refuse trades union membership where a closed shop applies was reinforced by the passing of the Employment Act in August 1980. Accordingly a worker can reject trades union membership if he/she genuinely objects on grounds of conscience.

As trades unions exist to further their members' aims, one of their main tasks is to try to increase the wages of their members. It is in this field that economic and political forces often collide. Many governments have tried in some way to control incomes in order to control inflation. Unions have, at various stages, been willing to support the government or been wholly antagonistic to such policy. The relative failure of incomes policies has often been used as an illustration of the extent of union power – there has grown a feeling that unions have too much power. Many feel that the unions' power to cripple the country has led to a stage where governments lose if they confront unions. The events leading to the first General Election of February 1974 and the election of 1979 are cited as evidence of this.

It was largely to control this perceived abuse of power that the 1979 Conservative Government introduced a number of pieces of legislation to restrict union power. The 1980 Employment Act placed limits on picketing, the 1982 Employment Act restricted the existence of closed shops, and the 1984 Trades Union Act insisted on secret ballots before industrial action and the need to ballot members in order to allow some union funds to be used for political activity. This latter provision was seen, by the Labour Party, as a party political action aimed at weakening the Labour Party.

The trades unions have had long and close links with the Labour Party; indeed, some were instrumental in the foundation of the Labour Party. Even now, much of Labour Party finance comes from subscriptions from the unions which are affiliated to the party. In such unions part of the members' subscription goes towards Labour Party finance unless an individual chooses to 'contract out'; in return delegates from the unions can attend the Labour Party Annual Conference (the governing body of the Labour Party) and have one vote for each union member, which can be cast in a block – hence the term 'block voting'. The block vote means that unions can out-vote individual members, about 6 to 1 and have their policies accepted as Labour Party policy. They can also affect the membership of the National Executive Committee which deals with the day-to-day running of the Party, by voting on their nominees.

It would be quite wrong to assume that the Labour Party is dominated by the unions; the parliamentary party has consistently fought for its right to pursue the policies not of conference but of the parliamentary party. The power struggle within the Labour Party which led to the expulsion of leading members of the Militant Tendency indicates the extent to which there is a divide between members of the parliamentary party and some members of the party outside parliament.

The limits to union power or influence appear to be the extent to which their power remains a negative one – to disrupt rather than to build, it is this type of highly visible action which gives the unions at least the appearance of having greater power than is possessed by employers. The period of Mrs Thatcher's administrations have been marked by a radical reduction in trades union power and influence. Trades unions have been kept very much 'at arm's length' on matters of industrial and economic policy.

Financial institutions
In any country which relies heavily upon trade and industry those institutions which control the flow of funds and credit will have great power. This is especially true in Britain where 'the City' plays a large part in determining the business confidence people feel and the likelihood of success being enjoyed by a new venture. At the same time it is not easy to see how the power of finance is used, certainly there does not appear to be any type of conspiracy of individuals wanting to use their power, although one might believe there was if one listened to certain left-wing Labour supporters. Again, it can be seen as individuals and groups reinforcing each other's ideas and creating a situation in which financial confidence is

high, leading to a feeling of success; or where financial confidence is low, leading to an unwillingness to finance new ventures. In the 1970s, with high inflation rates, high interest rates and curbs on profits, confidence was very low – and this had some effect on the prosperity enjoyed by Britain. In addition, the need for Britain to seek support from bodies such as the International Monetary Fund badly affected the willingness of banks to take risks. The Conservative Government White Paper on the economy, published in 1980, set out monetarist policies to 'remove the cancer of inflation'. Restriction of the money supply has been a key feature of inflation control in the 1980s. Government spending on welfare provision and private company subsidies has been curtailed, and by 1986 the inflation rate was under 3%. However, it seems that no radical measure is without cost – in this case the cost of high unemployment.

In conclusion we can see that the ability to influence, in whatever way, the economy of an advanced industrial society gives individuals and groups very great power. The power, though, does not rest exclusively with any one group at any one time. Each group has some power and at different times the balance of power may shift. Arguments which suggest that one group or other has too much power must be examined to determine what is meant by 'too much' power and whether a diminution of power would favour another group.

Military power

In many ways military power is the easiest type to see and to understand. TV pictures of British troops fighting in the Falklands, exercizing at the London airports, or even RAF aeroplanes flying overhead, demonstrate to us that there are organizations in our society which can use force should the need arise. The armed forces control the major part of the weaponry of Britain and, indeed, of most countries. This gives them tremendous potential power, but this power is seldom used directly. The threat of force is often sufficient deterrent. In many developing countries military power has been an active element in political struggle; the armed forces have been instrumental in replacing one government with another. The intervention of military personnel has led, in some Third World countries, to the establishing of military governments, for example in Nigeria in 1985.

The armed forces in most Western industrial nations seem unwilling to become involved directly in political struggles – they see their role as being subservient to those who control the government of the country. Military power gives way to political authority. Whether this deference to political authority is absolute is doubtful. In 1981 officers of the Spanish army took over the Cortes in an attempted coup, because they objected to government policy. Both Portugal and Greece must also be seen as potentially somewhat unstable in this respect.

Without a doubt the military in Britain could seize control since it has the expertise and the technology to do so, but the armed forces accept that the government has the authority (given by the people) to rule without direct military interference. This is not to say, however, that the military is without influence. Defence spending is one of the major items of expenditure of any British government, and the leaders of the military use their influence on government to gain the funds they require for weaponry. Fears of external threat can lead governments to very high levels of expenditure as can be seen by the cost of the Trident project in Britain.

The secondary position of the military in liberal democracies means that they should only act when authorized to do so by the political leaders of the country. The Falklands war of 1982 illustrates this point. The Falkland Islands were invaded by Argentina in April 1982 and the decision to defend the Islands by the use of force was taken by the government, not by the military. Only when government approval was given could the task force be sent and even then the rules of engagement were partly drawn up by politicians. It was a political decision as to when diplomatic initiatives had failed and when military options should be exercized.

The stability of parliamentary democracy in Britain has removed the need for direct military involvement in politics, except on rare occasions when instructed by the civil authorities to take action. Such stability allows the military to retain its traditional role, in reserve, ready to repel external aggression and to assist the police in the maintenance of internal law and order as, for example, in Northern Ireland.

Although the major task of the armed forces of most countries is to defend the nation against others and respond to political or military attacks, in some countries the prime purpose of the armed forces is to keep the civilian population subdued. Marxists would argue that the armed forces of all liberal democracies are part of the Repressive State Apparatus which also includes the legal system and the police. This Repressive State Apparatus exists to bolster up the Ruling Class by controlling, either directly or by threat, the majority of the population. The involvement of troops in industrial disputes is seen as a sign that the military is not neutral but exists to support a class society. It cannot be denied that at times the armed forces are used by the government to mitigate the effects of emergencies, both civil and industrial; but those in government would say that this is for the benefit of the population as a whole, not as a way of protecting their position.

Discussion point
If the military in politically stable countries is unwilling to step into politics, what protects such countries from the dangers which often cause the military to act in less politically stable countries?

Externally the armed forces of most countries share the same tasks, to defend the nation against others and to respond to political or military attacks. War is the ultimate test of a country's power and it is for this purpose that armed forces are kept (although in some countries it could be said that the prime purpose of the armed forces is to keep the civilian population subdued).

It is only in times of war and occasional civil unrest that military power is of great relevance in the advanced countries, but the possibility of the military defending the civil order adds strength to a political system.

In addition to these centres of power – political, economic and military – other institutions exert great influence and also have some degree of power. The education system acts to spread knowledge and to train young minds, and, to a considerable extent, to ensure conformity. With the mass media, the education system controls the flow of ideas and information we consider. This gives them great control over what ideas and information are seen as legitimate. Organized religion still exerts some power, and much authority, though over a declining proportion of the population. Pronouncements of leading churchmen are still of great importance and are widely reported.

Leading members of the judiciary have both great power and authority, for their pronoucements are also listened to with interest and are presented as authoritative. Once again it becomes clear that one cannot point to one group of people and say 'they alone have power'. In Britain power seems to be spread among many people.

The distribution of power in Britain

We have seen that various groups have some degree of power and this has led some people to argue that Britain remains democratic and stable because no one group or individual has overwhelming power – there is a constant competition between power groups which prevents one group from dominating, power is diffused throughout the political system. Another view holds that the competing groups do so on unequal terms – some are able to dominate others and to impose their wills on other groups. A third argument is that most of these people in positions of power share common backgrounds and beliefs and form one, not many groups – a ruling class. This approach implies that the beliefs which hold our leaders together are stronger than their differences. Each of these approaches has strong political implications – the first tends to be supported by conservatives – those people who support the present system whatever political party they belong to. The last view tends to be that of the 'extreme' left, whose members are highly critical of the present system. The second view can be embraced by those who hold both types of political view at various times.

1   Power is diffuse

In some ways this view can be likened to a sporting event, all the groups we have mentioned are in competition to win. In order to win power they must persuade the electorate to support them rather than the other competitors. To do this they generally try to show that they are working in the national interest and for the benefit of as many diverse groups in society as possible. The electorate, according to this view, act as the adjudicator in the competition. The group which achieves the widest appeal gains the victory. However, this simple observation becomes for politicians a precarious balancing act: they must 'feed' the voters enough positive evidence that their party will be the most effective in government but remain sufficiently non-committal so as to offend as few voters as possible and, at the same time, retain freedom of action should political power be won. Extreme parties which hold to rigid doctrines and policies deny themselves the flexibility which could make them more effective challengers to the major parties.

Not only is the diffusion of political power illustrated by the electoral strategy of major political parties but also by the restraining influences on governments once they are elected. Figure 4 indicates some of the influences and organizations which have acted as a brake on, or a spur to, government action in the past.

Figure 4   *Some influences which can restrain a government*

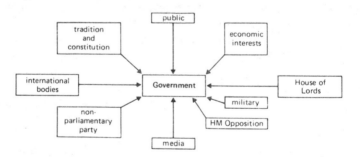

The contention, here, is that power is divided among many groups. The number of groups may increase and, following this line of argument, it could only strengthen the political system.

Discussion point
What are the disadvantages of such a wide distribution of power? Are there any advantages to be gained from power being concentrated?

2 Power is misused by some groups

This view sees power as entailing a responsibility; the need to act in a reasonable manner. From time to time groups are accused of abusing the power they have or of trying to increase their power. Trades unions are often singled out for criticism in this respect, for many feel that the balance between other powerful groups and trades unions has been altered to such an extent, that unions are able to control or dominate other groups and the public.

A similar type of criticism is sometimes levelled at the power of business, particularly by the left. Business concerns may be criticized if they refuse to invest, make people redundant or increase prices. Governments, of whatever party, are often accused, by their opponents, of acting in a high-handed fashion and pushing through policies which are unpopular.

Behind such claims often lie differences of political opinion over the role of government, business or unions and it is a convenient way to attack an opponent, to claim that he is acting outside the rules of the game, or that the rules favour him rather than oneself. Not all such criticisms can be explained in purely ideological terms for there are examples where the consensus appears to support the view that a group has acted irresponsibly.

The excesses of the miners' strike of 1984–5 where there were violent confrontations between the police and miners – and indeed where one working miner was killed by striking miners – persuaded many people that, whatever the strengths of the miners' case, they had overstepped the boundaries of acceptable behaviour.

To say that a group has 'too much' power involves a judgement as to what the proper function of the group is and whether such a function is being overstepped. For instance, is the true function of a union to better its members' position at any cost? If it is not, where can one draw the line as to what is acceptable or not? Is the true function of government to lead or to respond to what the electorate wants it to do? The answer to these and similar questions depends to a large extent upon one's view of the ideal balance of power in our society.

3   *Power is held by people who share similar backgrounds and beliefs*

In the 1983 Thatcher cabinet of twenty-one individuals, no fewer than seventeen had been to Oxford or Cambridge universities. The Labour cabinet of 1979 had twenty-four individuals, of whom all but one, Mr Callaghan, had been to a university. The majority of MPs have been to university, most to grammar or public schools, and most are drawn from non-manual occupations. The Conservatives have a higher proportion of landowners and businessmen than Labour, who have a higher proportion of teachers and journalists. The similarities between the backgrounds of MPs are more striking than the dissimilarities. In social terms the House of Commons is unrepresentative of the populace as a whole. About 40 per cent of the population of Britain are in non-manual (middle class) occupations and 60 per cent in manual (working class) occupations. This balance is not reflected in parliament. Such an imbalance is hardly surprising, though the job of MP is non-manual and therefore likely to attract the professional category.

According to many commentators the leaders of all parties show more in common with the leaders of other influential groups than they do with the people they represent. Top businessmen, civil servants, military leaders and politicians all *tend* to come from similar backgrounds and have shared similar paths through education. Many left-wing writers (particularly Marxists) argue that these shared backgrounds are reflected in shared values – ideas of what is important: and that the people occupying top positions will tend to view the world in a similar way and seek similar solutions to problems. These people could be seen to form the ruling class of our society, who actually control what happens in most major fields and who are able to pass their knowledge and positions on from generation to generation. If this is true, then the argument continues, the choice between Labour and Conservative is no choice at all. Both leadership groups are part of the same class who will act in very similar ways when in power. W.L. Guttsman in *The British Political Élite* attempted to show which were the positions of power in Britain. Figure 5 shows his conclusions.

Figure 5 *Membership of certain élite groups*

Elite group	Size Gross*	Net*
1 Members of the government	68	
2 MPs	630	730
3 Peers active in the House of Lords	100	
4 Highest Civil Service	169	169
5 Judiciary	77	77
6 Military leaders	319	319
7 Boards of nationalized industries	350	345
8 Industrial directorate a) top companies, capital £1million and over	2725	2450
b) medium companies, capital £200,000–£1million	6750	6100
9 Boards of major banks and insurance companies	422	340
10 Governors of major autonomous and semi-autonomous agencies	161	150
11 Principal government advisory committees	363	330
12 Leaders of science and learning	200	200
13 Leaders of major economic pressure groups	53	53
14 Trade union leadership	60	60
15 Spokesmen of the professions	40	40
16 Heads of churches	70	70
Total:	12,557	11,053

* Gross figures represent total positions available. Some individuals hold positions in more than one group; the net figure shows the total if these are taken into account.

Source: W. L. Guttsman, *The British Political Elite*, 1965

These people together number about 11,050 in total and
Guttsman concluded that:

There exists today in Britain a 'ruling class', if we mean by it a group
which provides the majority of those who occupy positions of power,
and who, in their turn, can materially assist their sons to reach
similar positions.

This view implies that power is very concentrated, always
upon the same class and never with the people. Others would
argue that shared social backgrounds do not necessarily result
in shared beliefs and that there is a real difference between the
groups competing for power.

Conclusion

Diffuse or concentrated – are we ruled by one class or is there a
constant competition for the favour of the public? This is one
of the central questions in political debate and we shall return
to it in the final chapter on Democracy. It is clear, though, that
as individuals we lack all but a small amount of power,
exercized at elections. In the Liberal Democracies of the West
most power resides in the hands of groups, mainly political
parties but also interest groups. It is a matter of judgement as
to whether these groups operate in their own interests or
whether they are a reflection of the popular will. Do frequent
elections and ease of membership of groups indicate popular
control, or do they hide the reality of unrepresentative, self-
seeking groups?

Essay questions

1   What are the forms of political opposition in the United
    Kingdom? How do these forms of political opposition
    affect the operation of the British system of government
    and politics? (JMB, June 1979)
2   'There is no such thing as absolute monopoly power.'
    Discuss. (Cambridge, Summer 1982)
3   Does the extension of the power of government justify the
    phrase 'Big Brother is watching us'? (Oxford, Summer
    1984)
4   If the only legitimate source of political authority is

election, what are the justifications for the House of Lords and the monarchy? (London, June 1982)

5 Can you justify inequalities in the possession and distribution of political power and influence? (London, June 1982)

6 Should back-benchers have more power than they have at present? (London, June 1984)

7 Has the Prime Minister only the semblance of power? (London, January 1986)

8 Compare the political power wielded by the leaders of industry and trades unions. (AEB Specimen Question 1986)

9 To what extent do the records of recent governments support the view that the power of the Prime Minister is determined by the unity of the Cabinet? (AEB Specimen Question 1986)

Short-answer questions

1 Distinguish what is meant by 'authority' and 'authoritarian'. (London, June 1978)

2 What power does the British Monarch have? (London, June 1984)

3 Distinguish between the concept of 'power' and that of 'authority'. (London, June 1985)

4 Distinguish between political influence and political power. (London, January 1986)
   Refer to Chapter 5 before attempting this question.

5 Distinguish between the power and authority of the House of Lords. (London, June 1986)

5 Pressure and influence

Throughout our lives we are expected to behave in certain ways, at home, at school or at work. Our actions are influencd by others who try to make it clear what they want us to do, they try to pressure us into doing what they desire. At the same time we also exert pressure upon others to act as *we* want them to. Examples might include persuading parents to extend the time when you are supposed to be home after a disco or convincing a teacher to limit the amount of homework he sets. A more extreme case would be the threat of a teenage girl to leave home if her parents do not allow her more personal freedom and recognize that she is growing up. These activities of persuading and influencing are means of exerting pressure to achieve some end either in a positive way, such as being able to do something you want to do, or in a negative way, such as dissuading somebody from doing what you do not want them to do.

The distinction between pressure and influence is a fine one. **Pressure** tends to be used to describe persuasive actions which are organized and which have some definite intent; thus parents are exerting pressure when they jointly try to persuade their child to clean up his room. **Influence** is less likely to be organized persuasion; indeed, often it is unintentional and unperceived. A pop star may have great influence over his fans even if he does not realize it; by his actions he may cause them to adopt new catch phrases, styles of dress and so on. Influence is closely related to authority whilst pressure is more closely related to power.

The methods by which we exert pressure are numerous and each situation may require us to use a different type of pressure. If you are trying to persuade a younger brother or sister to do something you may exert pressure by reference to age – 'I'm older than you, so do as I say' – or by threat of violence – 'Do as I say or I'll hit you'. Such methods would be inappropriate if you were dealing with parents, teachers or other adults. The pressure that we can exert depends to a large extent upon the amount of power and authority we have, thus teachers are often better able to persuade pupils to do what they want than are pupils to persuade teachers. Nevertheless, there are circumstances where pressure can be exerted successfully by people who have little power or authority. Broadly, these are circumstances where moral problems are concerned, in trying to show others that such a course of action is right and fair. In this respect an ability to articulate one's case is important, to be able to present it in a way that others will understand and respond to. The relative success of the Greenpeace Organization, who try to protect the environment, and particularly animal life, illustrates this point. Largely as a result of their activities there is now a total ban on whaling, although some countries may be ignoring this ban. Pressure, then, is not something which all people can exert with equal ability. Those in authority, the powerful, those who can articulate their demands in an attractive way, are better able to put forward their case than less favourably placed individuals and groups in society. Many people would argue that certain groups are too well able to exert pressure and that their ability to exert such pressure is a danger to democracy.

The individual and the group

Individuals in large scale industrial societies may lack sufficient knowledge to have a direct effect on the workings of large organizations, including the government, and for that reason may feel themselves to be powerless. This position is a paradoxical one for democracy is supposed to be a type of government which protects the rights of individuals, but it is clear that to do this it sets up structures which, though necessary, are at a distance from the people. Such structures are highly complex and rely on individuals with particular skills for their functioning and so become controlled by experts. The average citizen is not expert enough to influence such organizations and so must join with other individuals in groups which are capable of employing or using their own experts. One difficulty which then may affect such groups is that their experts may become distant from the very people they are supposed to be representing. Trades unions have had this criticism levelled at them in recent years: members may feel that the leadership is isolated from the rank and file.

The apparent lessening of the power of the individual does not mean that his rights have disappeared, merely that in our present, expert-orientated, form of society, the individual is less able to exert pressure as an individual. One can still attempt to influence by a number of means – writing to the local MP or to the newspapers. To be really effective, however, it is necessary for individuals to organize into groups. People banding together to support causes and/or for reasons of self-protection are a growing feature of modern society and are consulted by governments very frequently. Most people now belong to one or more of these groups, but such membership is usually of a passive kind involving group membership only, perhaps paying subscriptions, but rarely active participation in the work of the group. Despite this, individuals can become actively involved with group work, and indeed, some must if democratic action is to be enriched in terms of participation.

New students of politics find the world of group activity a confusing one peopled with pressure groups, interest groups, sectional interests, cause groups and a wealth of others. Much confusion arises from the terms themselves, which overlap in meaning. We shall attempt to dispel some of the confusion by referring throughout to interest groups rather than pressure groups as this latter term implies that the sole function of groups is to exert pressure. We shall see that this is not necessarily so for many groups. The main purpose of interest groups is to influence policy decisions, but may also perform other tasks for their members and for the wider public.

Interest groups are an essential part of the political process, for it would be impossible to imagine the political machine working without them. But not all groups involved in politics are interest groups. A distinction between political parties and interest groups would be helpful. Although political parties sometimes contain interest groups their aims are generally wider, as indicated in this definition by Jean Blondel in *Voters, Parties and Leaders*:

Interest groups differ from political parties by their aim, which is not to take power but only to exert pressure. They differ from parties by their objects, which are usually limited in scope. They differ from parties by the nature of their membership, which is often limited to one section in society.

If we adopt Blondel's approach then we can say that most interest groups are not interested in the whole of the political process and certainly do not want to gain power. If we consider a group such as the National Society for the Prevention of Cruelty to Children (NSPCC), its main aim is to protect children and to be concerned with legislation which affects children. Its membership is made up of people interested in child welfare but not necessarily in wider political issues. There is, of course, no question of the NSPCC wishing to seek governmental power.

The growth of group activity

All those who have held governmental office have been subject to some pressure, either by groups or individuals; decision-making which affects others will call forth some response from those affected and there have always been occasions when pressure has been exerted. While the scope of government activity was limited to a small number of functions such as internal law and order and external defence, very few groups emerged to exert pressure over decision-making. In the main, pressure tended to be exerted by individuals or by very loosely organized groups which formed for *ad hoc* purposes.

It was with the Industrial Revolution that government had to accept a major change in its role and function and government became involved in spheres of activity which affected the whole population in a way that had never been done before. Public health provisions, factory acts and compulsory education all became major concerns of government in the nineteenth century. These changes were in part due to the pressures exerted upon government by groups in society to be more responsive to the needs of people. Moreover, interest groups appeared. These trends will be further discussed in the final chapter. The movement of the government into the economy and its acceptance, particularly since the Second World War, of a very active role in controlling unemployment and inflation, means that most adults are daily reminded of government involvement in their lives. The growth of the welfare state to provide for the weak in society has been brought about by government becoming gradually, and sometimes reluctantly, more and more involved in matters which were previously thought to be outside its rightful scope.

The growth of mass democracy and increased government intervention brought with it the development of groups that wanted to influence such policy. Some of these groups, such as the Howard League for Penal Reform, were concerned largely with social matters and often had strong religious or moral overtones. Others, such as trades unions, had an economic base and can be seen as an economic reflection of the growing demand for working-class rights. From the first, some of these interest groups were looked on with caution, and indeed hostility by those in power. The early history of the trades union movement is a history of a constant struggle over legal and political obstacles. Gradually government has come to accept that in a mass democracy, which acknowledges the right to form groups, such groups can be of benefit to the working of government. As a result, many interest groups now have strong links with government and the principle of consultation of all interested groups has been accepted by most governments. The growth of local government activity has led to a similar growth of group activity at local level. Such groups tend to be less permanent than their national counterparts.

Types of interest groups

Interest groups vary enormously in size, from a few people who join together to pursue some common interest, to the millions of members in trades unions. Size is often associated with strength. However, another important factor is the membership of the group in relation to the number of people in a particular trade or profession who could seek membership. Thus the British Medical Association (BMA) is a strong group, because of the high proportion of doctors who belong to it. The Union of Shop Distributors and Allied Workers

(USDAW) whose members mainly work in the retail trade is a very large union but lacks the 'muscle' of other groups because it represents a relatively low proportion of retail workers. Another element in deciding strength is the status of such groups in the community at large. Doctors have a very high status and the community tends to look favourably on their needs. Shop workers have a lower status than doctors; this lack of status can be a drawback in winning public support.

Rather than classifying interest groups by size it is common to adopt definitions which refer to their aims – what they hope to achieve. Probably the best distinction to be made is between *promotional groups* and *protective groups*. Blondel defines the two thus: promotional groups 'want to promote a cause by appealing, not to a section, to a special group, but to everybody'. Protective groups 'defend a section in society'.

Promotional groups
These are sometimes called *cause groups*. Such groups are formed by people who want to put forward a particular cause, of whatever type. They seek to persuade people to support their cause in the hope of gaining strength or funds from such support. Promotional groups range over an enormous field of interest – from Friends of the Earth, the environmental protection group, to the NSPCC, the National Society for the Prevention of Cruelty to Children. Some groups, such as the Life campaign which opposes abortion, are controversial in their aims; others enjoy more widespread support – Oxfam, for example.

The diversity and number of promotional groups is perhaps their greatest weakness, for the public is under such pressure to support this or that group that they often respond apathetically or spasmodically. Government also labours under the same type of problem, exacerbated because promotional groups are often opposed in their aims by other promotional groups. Thus the supporters of abortion law reform are opposed by those who want the law to be retained in its present form. These, in turn, are opposed by those who want the law to be liberalized to allow abortion on demand. It is not surprising that the causes put forward by promotional groups often relate to those subjects which the government feels inclined to leave to Private Member's legislation.

It used to be said that promotional groups were less permanent than protective groups, that if they achieved their aims they would disband. One must now begin seriously to question this, as many groups appear to continue after their initial aims have been met, and adopt the role of monitoring government activity in their field of interest. Some groups are temporary but many are not.

Promotional groups are not representative in the formal sense. Membership may or may not include people who are affected by the activities of the group. The leaders of such groups usually emerge because of the time and energy they are willing to give to the cause. Their claim to represent is not based upon a formal system of voting by those interested or affected, but upon a perceived need to speak up for a deprived but inarticulate group in society. Oxfam, for instance, may claim to speak for the starving but in no real way has it a mandate to do so. Clearly the RSPCA could not possibly be representative in the strictest sense. The Child Poverty Action Group concerned with the protection of children, whilst effective, is not a representative body in the above sense. In a society where we place high value on organizations being representative this can be seen as a serious drawback, and sometimes leads to accusations that promotional groups are composed of 'do gooders' and 'busy bodies'. Such accusations are, on the whole, unjust, for promotional groups have the enormous benefit of being composed of committed and expert individuals.

The main characteristics of promotional groups are:

(*a*)   They are many and varied in size and aims.
(*b*)   They tend to have limited aims.
(*c*)   They usually disperse when a set of objectives has been achieved or irreversibly lost.
(*d*)   They tend not to be representative bodies.

Exercise
Look in a newspaper for an example of a promotional group at work. Keep a diary of its progress, how successful is it?

Protective groups
These are sometimes also called *sectional interests* because they exist to represent the interests and aims of a distinct

section of the community. It is protective groups which are most often in the public eye, both because they have the 'muscle' to exert pressure successfully, and because they have been built by government into a consultative framework for proposals which affect them. Protective groups are the largest of the interest groups, the greatest of all being the Trades Union Congress with nearly 10 million members.

Clearly the most publicized protective groups are trades unions and the Confederation of British Industry, which can claim to speak with an authoritative voice on matters which concern them. The range of protective groups can be extended to include the Automobile Association, the Law Society, and the British Medical Association.

Protective groups are often controlled by leaders who have to submit themselves for election or approval by the membership. So such groups can claim to be democratically organized. Their membership is composed of a high proportion of those involved in a particular occupation and therefore eligible to join, for instance, the National Union of Mineworkers. In such circumstances, government and other interested bodies find the expertise and representative nature of protective groups provides the best focus for consultation when any changes are proposed. It is worth noting, however, that the extent to which trades union leaders really represent their rank and file members is a controversial issue.

Protective groups tend to be permanent bodies which often develop ancillary functions to those concerned purely with affecting policy formulation. Trades unions organize social events for their members, educational courses, health facilities, insurance and many other benefits besides acting as negotiators on pay and conditions. The motoring organizations provide many services to members in addition to protecting their interests from harm; indeed it is probably true that in their case the interest group activity is a relatively small part of their organizational activities. Some members may not know that the group acts as an interest group. Professional groups such as the Law Society and British Medical Association impose standards of conduct on their members and act in a disciplinary fashion where they feel their code of conduct has been breached.

Protective groups, then, generally have the following

characteristics:
(*a*)   They include the largest of all interest groups.
(*b*)   They tend to be permanent and, to some extent, demo-
        cratically organized.
(*c*)   They often carry out other functions besides those of
        exerting pressure.
(*d*)   Because of their size, permanence and expertise, they
        are often consulted by government.
(*e*)   They are the most effective type of pressure group.

The distinction between promotional and protective groups
must be treated with some caution because there are many groups
which do not fit exactly into either category. Where, for instance,
would one place the Campaign for Homosexual Equality?

Focuses of pressure

Just as interest groups differ in size, membership and aim,
they differ in where they decide pressure will be most
effective, and the best methods to achieve their aims. In
general, most interest groups focus on three major areas,
though some restrict themselves solely to one or two. The
major areas for focus are:
(*a*)   government and Civil Service
(*b*)   parliament and individual Members of Parliament
(*c*)   the public

In addition to these areas the mass media are a focus of
group activity, but they also act as interest groups. We shall
discuss the role of the media later in this chapter.

Government and Civil Service
In many ways this is the most effective target of most interest
groups. In the twentieth century the British system has seen a
gradual shift of power from the legislature to the executive and
this has meant that parliament is no longer as important in the
decision-making process as it once was. The executive is now
able, within certain bounds, to carry out its intentions as it can
normally be assured of a parliamentary majority because of
the party discipline which exists in parliament.

Decisions are increasingly taken by ministers on the advice
of civil servants and presented to parliament for approval. To
be able to influence the decision-making process is likely to be

the most effective way of achieving the aims of a group. Ministers, though, are protected from too much pressure by their civil servants who control the flow of information. This makes civil servants also a target for pressure. The concept of civil service neutrality means that civil servants should not act in an openly political way, but as they do provide information for ministers and policy alternatives for consideration, this gives them great influence and even greater power. Mr Tony Benn has described this growth in power as a major threat to democracy.

It is difficult to assess accurately the extent and effectiveness of pressure applied in this area. Certainly some groups can gain fairly easy access to a minister's office but others have great difficulty in presenting their case to ministers. Promotional groups often complain that they find great difficulty in putting their case as effectively as they would want.

Interest groups which have proven expertise and which will be materially affected by government proposals are naturally consulted by government, indeed such groups as the National Farmers' Union must by law be consulted. Where consultation exists it is difficult to gain a true picture of its effectivenes, but the Labour Government's 'Social Contract' with the trades union movement from 1974–9 shows how close the links between government and interest groups can become.

Parliament and individual MPs
The legislature is responsible for enacting new statutes and the volume of such activity has increased dramatically over the past thirty years. Interest groups realize both that MPs are part of the legislative process, and that their position enables them to draw to the attention of the public, and the government, matters which concern them. To have the support of a back-bench MP, particularly a well-known one, is a great advantage to an interest group.

There are three main ways in which MPs are subject to the actions of interest groups; through sponsorship, through personal interest, and through lobbying carried out by interest groups and individuals.

A very high number of candidates, almost all of them Labour, are sponsored by organizations at General Elections. Trades unions are the main organizations involved in this

activity, particularly the National Union of Mineworkers and
the Transport and General Workers' Union. In the 1983
General Election, some 144 Labour candidates were so
sponsored. Since sponsorship usually involves paying the
election expenses of candidates, clearly some return on this
investment is anticipated. What this return may be is
sometimes difficult for the sponsors to assess. Clearly unions
will only sponsor candidates who they feel to be sympathetic
towards them and who will support them in parliament. Some
union leaders have gone further than this and claim that
sponsored MPs should be the representatives of the union in
parliament. Such a view is unpopular with MPs; indeed in
October 1975, Mr Arthur Scargill of the Yorkshire NUM was
found guilty of contempt of parliament for trying to force
sponsored MPs to follow NUM policy.

In a similar way many Conservative and some Labour MPs
have strong links with business. Some are employed as
consultants to firms and interested groups, being paid for
giving political advice. How far the receipt of monetary
rewards imposes pressure on an MP to support the donor is
open to question. Concern over the effect of MPs' outside
interests led in 1975 to the setting up of a register of MPs'
interests. Only one MP, Mr Enoch Powell, has consistently
refused to register.

The second way MPs come into contact with group pressure
is by having an interest in a particular area of policy. Most
MPs have areas which interest them more than others and
their knowledge often involves them with interest group
activity. MPs such as Jack Ashley, who is concerned at the
plight of the deaf, and Greville Janner, concerned with the
handicapped, are of great benefit to interest groups through
their ability to put forward cases in the media and parliament.

The other main way in which MPs are influenced is by
lobbying: direct persuasion being used on MPs by interest
groups, or by individuals. Lobbying in Britain is not so well
developed as it is in the USA, where Representatives and
Senators are the targets of highly professional lobbyists
whose task is to persuade them to support one cause or
another.* Lobbying in Britain is still done on a more amateur
basis, although the number of public relations firms specializ-
ing in parliamentary activity appears to be growing. Letters,

petitions and personal meetings are used by constituents and interest groups to try to influence an MP and gain his support. Larger groups, and foreign countries, try to enlist support by providing material, literature and arranging 'fact finding' trips. The extent to which such activities are ethical is a purely personal judgement: should an MP accept free leaflets, free dinners, free trips? Where should one draw the line?

Discussion point
Should an MP's sole task be to put forward his constituents' interests or is it acceptable for him to be involved in interest-group activity?

The public
For a protective pressure group, public opinion is of less direct relevance than it is for promotional groups. We have seen that protective groups are better able to put their case directly to the executive and legislature. Public opinion is difficult to mobilize and is uncertain in its effect. The only time the majority of the electorate is involved simultaneously in any political activity is during general elections. It is unlikely that the activities of interest groups will deflect large numbers of voters from traditional party loyalties. In the periods between General Elections governments need not be so eager to fit in with the wishes of the public, particularly as it is usually unclear as to what these wishes are.

Despite these problems many interest groups concentrate on the public for a number of reasons. One of the recurring problems which faces the majority of groups is the availability of funds. The process of influencing decisions is a costly one and many groups seek public donations towards their work. With those groups which operate as charities, such as Oxfam, War on Want and Help the Aged, money is required to pay for the activities of relieving suffering and this is raised by flag days, charity shops and events such as Band Aid and Sport Aid.

* The Federal Election Campaign Act 1974, as modified by certain amendments in 1976, allowed special interest groups to set up *Political Action Committees* (PACs) to raise money for candidates. PACs are now a force in US politics, and allow the sponsoring interest group a fair measure of political leverage on the sponsored candidate. In election year 1984, business corporation PACs raised $127 million, while Labour union PACs raised $53 million.

Many groups also see their role as one of educating the public to support their cause, or in some cases to make them aware that a problem exists. Groups provide material for educational bodies of all sorts. The large groups have educational departments which can provide speakers and literature to interested people. The student of politics can often gain valuable material by writing to these groups. A major concern of many groups is to build up a body of public support and through it to bring pressure to bear on MPs or the government; groups often try to produce petitions, encourage a large number of people to write to their MPs and organize demonstrations and other types of activity to show that concern exists.

Although these focuses of activity have been presented as separate, they are in fact interlinked and most groups tend to use a mixture of more than one of these methods in order to achieve their ends. To do this requires considerable organizational skill and group activity is becoming increasingly professional in its approach. This again means that those sections of the community which lack such skills may be at a disadvantage if they do not have an expert group to support them.

The mass media

The influence of the mass media, radio, television and newspapers, on the formation of attitudes and changing opinions is a matter of considerable conjecture. What is clear is that these media are the main methods of political communication for the bulk of the population. Through them we hear news and are able to comment and form our judgements about political matters.

Both the British Broadcasting Corporation and the Independent Broadcasting Authority are required, by the terms of their charters, to present political issues in a balanced fashion. This often takes the form of giving equal opportunity to members of the major parties to put forward their views. In addition to interviews on television and radio programmes, major political parties are allowed time for party political broadcasts to put over their partisan viewpoints. At the time of a General Election some of the smaller parties may be entitled to make one or more party political broadcast.

During the 1983 General Election campaign, for example, the National Front, British National Party and the Ecology Party made such broadcasts. Despite this many people have expressed concern that the broadcasting authorities do not act in a neutral enough way: individual views are rarely heard on television or radio, interest groups have very little time to put forward their case and certain views are never heard on the broadcasting media, or are treated in an unbalanced way if they are. Extreme political parties often accuse the broadcasting authorities of a bias against them, this is especially true if the group is one which wants to change the existing political system. There has been continuing pressure on the authorities, for instance, not to put forward the case of terrorist groups in Northern Ireland. In July 1985, the BBC Board of Governors cancelled the transmission of a television programme which included interviews with Mr Martin McGuiness, a leading supporter of Sinn Fein and, it was said, a leading member of the IRA. The cancellation was thought to have been caused by government pressure, the decision having been reached after Mr Leon Brittain, the Home Secretary, asked the BBC to cancel the programme for reasons of security. The programme was later broadcast in an amended form.

In October 1986 Conservative Party Chairman, Mr Norman Tebbitt, forwarded a highly critical report to the BBC. It alleged pro-Libyan bias in the reporting of US bombings of that country.

Discussion point
Should all groups and individuals have equal opportunity to present their case on the media? What justifications could there be for limiting such opportunities?

National daily newspapers are not so concerned with neutrality. They perceive their role as twofold. First, to present the factual side of news and, second, to offer comment and opinion on such news. All newspapers have some sort of 'leader column' where their editorial view is presented. In Britain the majority of the press support, to a greater or lesser degree, the Conservative Party. Only the *Daily Mirror* has consistently supported Labour. *The Times* remains rather aloof from party politics but the other papers are fairly consistently Conservative.

Clearly most people are subject to some kind of political influence from their newspapers (see Butler and Stokes, *Political Change in Britain*), but again it is not clear whether people read newspapers *because* of their political beliefs, or whether the newspapers *create* political beliefs. In some cases there is doubt as to whether the readership even appreciate the political leanings of their newspapers. This major vehicle of political communication can sometimes also be used by individuals and groups to express their views, for instance, through the letter columns, but generally there is little two-way communication. As with other forms of pressure and influence the media use the power of experts to persuade the public.

Although there are exceptions, on the whole the mass media tend to support the present system, showing its imperfections but implying that alterations to it are dangerous or impractical. Radical solutions to problems, if they are presented at all, are described as being the product of muddled thinking, or condemned outright.

Exercise
From a recent newspaper can you find an example of trivializing an important issue?

Some problems of pressure and influence

So far we have seen group pressure as largely replacing individual pressure, and that certain groups and ideas are more likely to be presented as reasonable and acceptable by the media. We have also seen that there is a distinction to be drawn between interest groups and political parties. These generalizations remain, but recently other problems have been identified which upset this analysis.

The first problem concerns the distinction between parties and interest groups. There are some parties which see their role at present as being to change attitudes rather than to expect to gain power. The National Front, while wanting to gain power eventually, fielded 303 candidates in the 1979 General Election and 60 in the 1983 General Election, partly in order to gain access to the media for their opinions. Similar tactics were adopted in 1983 by the British National Party and the Ecology Party (now the Green Party). The difference of *intent* is important here for the methods used by pressure groups and political parties are often the same. In the late 1960s and during the 1970s many ratepayers' groups were established to monitor rate increases proposed by local councils. At first these were largely promotional groups, supporting the cause of low rates and sensible spending. Some then became protective groups – well-organized 'watch-dogs' to monitor local government in the long term. Others then put up candidates for local election with some successes. So one can see that ratepayers' associations can no longer be bracketed into one particular slot. They operate in a variety of ways: as promotional groups, protective groups or sometimes political parties.

Some groups have developed a strange relationship with government whereby they act almost as government agencies, receiving government support in order to pursue their aims. The Royal Society for the Prevention of Accidents (ROSPA) falls within this category. It both presses government for better safety laws and receives government help in order to educate the public and industry. Government can use pressure groups, then, as a way of improving communication. When this happens the links between pressure groups and government become highly complex; it is not easy to fit this in with the simple analysis that has been presented earlier in the chapter.

Perhaps one of the most serious shortcomings of the traditional view of pressure in Britain is the extent to which it implies that groups share a common purpose. In many cases this is not true as there may be disagreement within groups and organizations as to the way they should further their aims or, indeed, what these aims are. There is strong internal disagreement, for instance, within trades unions over what policies should be followed. Within other groups there are power struggles between competing groups. It is within political parties that this becomes most evident. There are well defined interest groups within both main political parties competing for supremacy. Within the Labour Party, for example, one can see a variety of competing groups whose view of where the Labour Party should go are very different. In the first half of the 1980s this was clearly seen by the debate as to the place of Militant Tendency within the party. Its supporters claimed that it was simply a group of like-minded individuals who were primarily Labour Party members. Its detractors claimed that Militant was a party which was trying to gain control of the Labour Party and turn it away from its traditional values and policies. The power struggle that followed led to the expulsion of leading members of Militant from the party and the declaration that membership of Militant was incompatible with Labour Party membership. To see the Labour Party, or the Conservative Party, as uniform bodies is, then, a mistake. Political parties can be said to comprise of conflicting and competing interests, which come together and remain stable so long as internal divisions are minimized.

A similar argument can also be extended to government itself. Not only is there disagreement between government members, there is perhaps a clearer division of interests between government departments. Departments may develop their own corporate view of their role and have a collective view on policy matters, and may have to compete with other departments if this view is to succeed. The Treasury is thought to be very successful in such activity, imposing its will on other departments. The final problem to be considered concerns those groups or individuals who try to exert pressure by extreme means: where should they be located within the political process? We have already mentioned the IRA and they provide a useful example. Wanting, as they do, an end of British involvement in Ulster they see their role as freedom fighters trying to liberate their country. To the vast majority in the United Kingdom they are terrorists to be stamped out. We must refer again to the question of when it is justifiable to break the law: is violent or unlawful pressure always wrong?

Conclusion

The web of pressure is not merely one group or an individual attempting to pressure another group or individual but a complex of cross-pressures. Within such a web it is difficult to decide who has caused what to happen and so the effectiveness of group or individual pressure is open to doubt. What is not open to doubt is the extent to which interest groups have become an integral part of the political process, essential for the smooth operation of our democracy. The supporters of the growth of such groups argue that without them it would be impossible to maintain a dialogue with government and others in power. However, if left unwatched, such groups would be allowed to act in ways which would increase the distance between governors and governed.

Those worried by the growth of groups argue that they have led to the individual being unable to have any influence on those in power. The need for expert to talk to expert means that the average member of the public is incapable of presenting his case to the powerful. They would also point out that whilst interest groups are useful to the well-organized sections of the community, to those with less ability to organize they are of little benefit.

Essay questions

1 To what extent are leaders of pressure groups:
   a) responsive to;
   b) representative of,
   their members? (AEB Specimen Question 1986)
   Read Chapter 6 before attempting this question.
2 'Some matters are too sensitive to be left to the normal play of party and pressure group politics.' Discuss this statement in the light of some recent issues. (JMB, June 1979)
3 Make a case for the activities of pressure groups, and a case against them. (London, January 1981)
4 'Pressure groups can be seen as performing a number of valuable functions within the political system.' What are these functions? (Oxford, Summer 1982)
5 'The problem in Britain today is not that pressure groups are too powerful but that they have too little say in government.' Discuss. (Oxford, Summer 1985)
6 Have pressure groups any significant part to play in the British political system? (Cambridge, Summer 1985)
7 Discuss the view that pressure groups render Britain ungovernable. (London, January 1982)
8 'Government by agreement with pressure groups is now an essential feature of British government.' Discuss. (London, January 1983)

9 'The main problem with powerful pressure groups in Britain is how to relate them to the public interest.' Discuss. (London, June 1983)
10 Do pressure groups prevent efficient government? (London, January 1986)
11 In what sense is the Civil Service itself a pressure group? (London, June 1986)

Short-answer questions

1 Distinguish between 'promotional' and 'sectional' pressure groups. (London, June 1979)
2 Define two main types of pressure groups in Britain. (London, June 1981)
3 Distinguish between political parties and pressure groups. (London, January 1982)
4 What are the main types of pressure group? (London, June 1982)
5 Distinguish between small parties and large pressure groups. (London, January 1985)
6 Why are some pressure groups considered undemocratic? (London, June 1986)

6 Representation and responsibility

Any book on basic political concepts would be incomplete without a consideration of the ideas of representation and responsibility. These ideas are of crucial importance both in the history of political thought and in the way they are applied within many political systems today. Wherever political discussions take place these terms are often used, and therefore one might be forgiven for thinking that everybody is clear about what they mean. Yet both these concepts, as used in a political context, have different meanings which deserve closer attention.

There are many reasons why individuals claim their worthiness to **represent** the many. Professor Crick puts it this way:

Historically most governments claimed to represent the will of the gods or of God. Others have claimed the authority because they are representative of a race, or a caste, a tribe or a family, a class or a nation; or of traditional areas of property, interests, the 'general will', the Party, the People or of individuals. And all of the claims can be put either in the form that representation is a mandated delegation or else a responsible discretion.

Representatives can be seen as a reflection of the ideas of their supporters who must put forward the views of those they represent, that is, they are *delegates*. Conversely they can be seen as individuals with some gifts which they exercise for the benefit of their supporters, whether or not the supporters agree with particular actions, the representative is expected to use his discretion. It is important to discover what are the attributes upon which individuals claim, and are sometimes given, **authority** to represent the people. Moreover, what does **responsibility** mean in this context?

Representation

There are three definitions which shed the most light on the idea of representation:

1 *The idea that a person or a group of people is representative or typical of a larger group or community.* Such a person or group is identified as *representative* because it reflects the characteristics of the larger group. Sociologists use the word in this sense when they carry out surveys with the co-operation of what is described as a *representative sample* of people. Dennis Kavanagh in his article 'Political recruitment', makes this observation on represenativeness:

> The Prime Minister will also wish his Cabinet to be broadly representative of the main interests in the party. He will want a national figure for the Scottish and Welsh Offices, at least one woman, and so on. Because the Labour Party more obviously contains political factions the Labour leader must also seek a balance between the political wings.

MPs in both major parties have been criticized for being *unrepresentative*, that is, *untypical* of the people they represent. Whether MPs should or could be representative in terms of background, education and so forth is not the main point here, but rather that *typicality* is one possible meaning of representation. In his book, *Representatives and Responsible Government*, Professor A. H. Birch has this to say:

> Critics sometimes suggest that the House of Commons would be improved if it were a social microcosm of the nation, but this is a doubtful proposition. It is extremely unlikely that a process of free election would ever yield members who constituted a cross-section of electors, just as it is unlikely that a representative sample can be obtained by asking for volunteers.

2 *A second important use of the word representation is to denote the function of an agent or delegate. A representative in this sense acts to safeguard and promote the interests of an individual or group.* How such representatives are chosen and how much freedom they have to operate are not of primary importance in this definition; of much greater importance is the function of preserving and promoting the interests of the person, group or organization they represent. Barristers,

advocates, commercial travellers and foreign ambassadors are all *representatives* in the sense outlined above. The spokesman of interest groups act as representatives when they are consulted by government departments or royal commissions. In the last decade controversy has revolved around one such group of representatives – trades union leaders, who have been consulted by successive administrations on industrial and economic policies and have thereby gained a more elevated position in the process of decision-making.

3 *A third use of the term is clearly expressed by Raymond Williams in his book* Keywords:

Represent [has acquired] a range of senses of making present: in the physical sense of presenting oneself or another to some person of authority; but also of making present in the mind and of making present to the eye, in painting and in plays.

In terms of discussion about representative democracy, which is more closely examined in Chapter 8, Raymond Williams provides this as one definition of a representative system:

the periodic election of persons who will continually represent [make present] the views of those who elected them.

To represent in this way, therefore, is to be a mouthpiece for some electors by expressing their opinions in the sense of definition 2, but it is something more.

Edmund Burke saw the need to make clear a distinction between two interpretations of the concept of representation in his famous address to the electors of Bristol in 1774. His distinction was drawn between a representative and a delegate.

A *representative*, he says, is one who stands for and speaks on behalf of another person or group. In addition such a person is chosen to exercise his own judgement on issues which come before the assembly to which he has been elected. Therefore this representative is more than the mouthpiece of his constituents, he is an assessor of issues who is elected to exercise his own judgement. In theory this judgement is exercised by a representative in accordance with the best interests of his constituents and therefore this interpretation is most closely allied to definition 2 given above.

A *delegate*, Burke concludes, is expressly elected by the people to articulate their views. It follows from this, that a delegate's official comments could be declared unrepresentative of the opinions of those who elected him. This description is most closely aligned with definition 3 above.

What can be drawn from this analysis? Certainly different views on representation are not always easily distinguishable and the difficulty is compounded by changing usage. The British experience illuminates one way representation can be embodied within a political system.

Elections of some kind are usually associated with the implementation of a representative system. Simply stated, it is the idea that the **power** and **authority** conferred upon a representative should be given by the people. For the representative, election to such a special position carries with it an *obligation* to the electors. It is worth noting, however, that being elected to office cannot be taken as the only criterion for defining a representative. Many American judges are elected but do not represent electors. The Pope is elected by the College of Cardinals but does not represent them.

The 650 MPs now returned to the British House of Commons are the elected representatives of the people. The nature of their representation has long been the focus of much debate. The idea of **consent** is pertinent here. Within each constituency it is the consent of the majority of electors which is sought in the return of one MP from a number of candidates put forward by different political parties. A unanimous verdict is almost impossible to achieve and therefore the opinion of the majority is accepted under present arrangements. After the election the chosen MP becomes the representative of all those in his constituency, whether they voted for or against him or abstained.

The picture so far presented makes no mention of one crucial political development: the emergence of strong, well-disciplined national parties. This factor alone has changed the basis of the British representative system. The late R.H.S. Crossman in his introduction to *The English Constitution* by Walter Bagehot has made this assessment:

In Bagehot's day, the private member was genuinely free to defy the whip, genuinely responsible to his own conscience, and his constituents. ... It was this independence of the private member that gave the Commons its collective character and made it the most important check on the executive. Now the prime responsibility of the member is no longer to his conscience or to the elector, but to his party. Without accepting the discipline of the party he cannot be elected, and if he defies that discipline, he risks political death. . . . Party loyalty has become the prime political virtue required of an MP, and the test of that loyalty is his willingness to support the official leadership when he knows it to be wrong.

Many believe that the Burkeian interpretation of representation has been irreversibly undermined because now the over-riding obligation of an MP is to his party machine. The present day role of the US congressman can be more closely identified with that of a nineteenth-century British MP than it can be with an MP today. For historical reasons the American party system is much weaker than in Britain and therefore congressional candidates are less dependent for election upon a national party machine, but more dependent upon their constituents. In terms of representation, therefore, constituents' interests take priority over party interests.

If the traditional idea of representation has been demoted in the British system, what has replaced it? A. H. Hanson and Malcolm Walles tender this analysis in *Governing Britain*:

Burke's address to the electors of Bristol has little relevance today. MPs owe to the electorate not so much their judgement as their loyalty to the party label, that took them to Westminster. Only through parties can one attempt a crude approximation of the 'wishes of the electorate' and at the same time hold responsible those to whom the power to govern is accorded. A significant reduction in party discipline might well produce the series of shifing coalitions that are a feature of the American Congress: the task of the electorate would be made more difficult, the fixing of responsibility well-nigh impossible.

This analysis may be pessimistic in that it tends to reduce the MP to a party supporter only. In many cases, though, MPs do exercise their own judgement and go against the wishes of their party. Nevertheless, it is true to say that in the main MPs seem to see their major identifying characteristic as being the party they belong to, and that it is unusual for an MP to consistently break with the wishes of his party, particularly when those wishes coincide with the views of his electorate.

The idea of **responsibility** has been introduced and it is to
this concept we will turn shortly. It is clear, however, that the
nature of representation is still a matter of controversy. The
Labour Party has been particularly prone to such controversies,
with constituency parties insisting on the right to have the
ability to decide whether or not to re-select sitting MPs. This
ability was seen, by some MPs, as having direct implications
on their role as representatives.

Exercise
Summarize the three ideas of representation mentioned
earlier in the chapter. Which do you find most convincing?

Responsibility

The term responsibility has been used in two different ways in
the previous section. Professor Crick refers to 'responsible
discretion' and Hanson and Walles mention the 'fixing of
responsibility' by the electorate upon those who govern. From
this it is possible to differentiate three uses of the term.

1 *A common use of the term 'responsible' and one which
encompasses the notion of 'responsible discretion' is accurately
summed up in the word responsiveness.* Those who are chosen
to represent are expected to be sensitive to the needs and
wishes of their constituents. This is one criterion by which
many voters assess a 'good' MP. 'Surgeries' or 'clinics' are
usually held by MPs on Saturday mornings so that they are
able to keep in touch with their constituents' needs and so that
they are seen to be **responsible** in this way. It is worth noting
that although this is a valid view of responsibility it is
necessary to weigh its substance against the independence of
an MP's role and his over-riding loyalty to his party.

Governments which are *responsive* follow, as a matter of
convention, the idea that they ought to listen to, and take note
of, the views of different groups within society before devising
and implementing policies. This provides one dividing line
between liberal–democratic regimes, which strive to live by
this principle, and authoritarian regimes which do not. An
authoritarian government may also respond to the wishes of
the people but only if it suits its purpose to do so. Generally

such a government stresses centralized power and control often at the expense of responsiveness.

2 *A second use of the term 'responsible' implies the idea of accountability.* This is a particular feature of the British political system. In accordance with this, certain political mechanisms are created whereby elected and some non-elected government officials are obliged to remain answerable to the people for their actions or inaction. Regular elections are one such mechanism at which time former MPs seeking re-election, not only woo the electorate by pledges to fight for future improvements, but also stand on the quality and effectiveness of their past representation. The public may be better able to judge such quality of representation since the introduction of radio broadcasting of parliament which enables the public, for the first time, to regularly hear MPs in action on their behalf.

At the highest level of government in Britain two well-tried conventions still have an impact, though less in recent years. The convention of:

(*a*) Collective Cabinet Responsibility binds ministers to present a united front in public on decisions made in cabinet, even though individual ministers may disagree with a decision privately. This being so, the cabinet takes collective praise or blame for the outcome of cabinet decisions.

(*b*) Individual Ministerial Responsibility identifying the minister in charge of a government department as the person answerable for the work of that department. The constitution provides for elected representatives, MPs, to hold ministers accountable through such procedures as 'Question Time' and committee hearings. (See Chapter 2 for a fuller discussion of these conventions.)

The whole question of responsibility in terms of accountability is hotly debated both inside and outside parliament. The argument revolves around the growth of the *bureaucracy* in the twentieth century. The army of civil servants needed to carry out an increasing governmental workload has had to equip itself with sophisticated modern techniques in order to cope. Cost analysis, and statistical research with the aid of complex computers, for example, indicate the technical skills now required for a modern government to function. Such a situation puts a distance of expert knowledge and know-how

between skilled civil servants appointed for a working life-
time and elected representatives many of whom hold office for
only a few years. How can MPs be fully effective, if they do not
have and are unable to acquire, the expertise to understand
what is going on? Difficulties are compounded by a tradition of
secrecy surrounding the work of Whitehall. In Britain
legislation, particularly the Official Secrets Act, prevents the
dissemination of official information, but this not only covers
genuinely sensitive areas on such grounds as national security,
but also minor matters which, it is suggested, would be quite
harmless even if they were to become public knowledge.

For the purpose of our studies it is important to emphasize
the difficulties in striking a balance between the requirements
of the public and MPs on the one hand, and the bureaucracy
on the other, in relation to the notion of responsibility. Many
reforms have been proposed to make ministers and senior civil
servants more accountable to parliament. Two of these are
worthy of particular attention.

The 1979 Conservative administration steered through the
establishment of fourteen new 'watch-dog' committees of MPs
to watch over every Whitehall department. These committees
covered agriculture, defence, education, employment, energy,
environment, foreign affairs, home affairs, industry and trade,
social services, transport, Welsh affairs, Scottish affairs and
all treasury matters. Many observers were initially sceptical
about the effectiveness of these committees but most now feel
that they do a useful job in checking government activity. It is
perhaps a sign of their usefulness that they seem to be less
bound by party political loyalties than was originally feared.

A second reform suggested is to pass a Freedom of
Information Act. This would give the public the right of access
to non-classified material. Such legislation has already been
enacted in the USA and Sweden. However, even if the principle
were agreed, the high cost of implementation would be a major
stumbling block, though a reform of this kind would enable the
public to be better informed and MPs to be better equipped to
fulfil their role as government 'watch-dogs'.

3   *A third interpretation of 'responsibility' rests more heavily
than the other two upon the notion of 'moral obligation'. It is the
expectation that individuals who hold the trust of the people*

carry out their work wisely and with integrity. A nurse has this kind of responsibility for a patient, as does a teacher for a student. Holders of high office also have this kind of responsibility, which may mean unpopularity at times. Lord Hailsham used the term in this sense in his speech on the Budget in 1962:

When a Government has to choose between a run on the pound and its own popularity, it has only one choice it can make. It makes it unwillingly. It must face unpopularity, loss of by-elections and even, if need be, defeat at a later General Election. This is the price of responsible government.

It may have been this notion of responsible government which led the 1979 and 1983 Thatcher administrations to implement considerable cuts in public expenditure affecting such key areas as social services and education. They argued that responsible (wise) government was the application of policies which would eventually enable Britain to live within her means. This entailed a boost to manufacturing industry particularly in the private sector, accompanied by a severe reduction in central and local government spending. It was, it seems, a matter of getting one's house in order, with the primary target of balancing the household budget. The argument is persuasive because the Conservatives claimed they had a *mandate* to follow through the proposed policies contained in their 1979 election manifesto. To the Conservative Government it was not only a matter of being responsible in the sense of applying what, in its view, are sensible and wise policies, but also of being responsive to the wishes of the majority of people as expressed through the ballot box.

Condemnation of government policies is often designed to reveal how irresponsible they are. For example it was asserted, particularly by the Labour Party, that the Thatcher Governments had not acted wisely, most notably on the question of public expenditure cuts. Critics feared that reductions in spending forced upon local authorities by central government resulted in less than adequate community services. The mid-1980s were marked by growing criticism that state services were becoming run down through inadequate funding. Teachers and administrators in the state school sector claimed that equipment was in short supply and buildings required repair. Those in the hospital service asserted that cuts reduced the standard of health care – delays in non-emergency treatment and in some health areas too few beds to meet demand. Those who would suffer most hardship because of such measures were ordinary people, and this, critics claimed, was far from responsible government.

Clearly the criteria according to which government actions are judged to be responsible or irresponsible *do* vary. What is the wisest course of action in a given situation is very often a matter of debate. Yet governing with wisdom and integrity does imply policies which are consistent. For example, in the fight against inflation, a government would be accused of inconsistency if it applied statutory limits on wage increases and yet had no policy to curb excessive price rises.

Discussion point

How would you judge whether a system ensured responsible and representative government?

A final comment

The perception of representation and responsibility held by those inside and outside government is a mixture of traditional and recent interpretations. When examining political issues it emerges that varying weight is attached to the different interpretations of these two concepts. Nevertheless, they are invaluable for an analysis of any liberal–democratic system. The concept of **democracy** will be explored in the final chapter, but it would be helpful here to draw a comparison or two between the British and American systems which are variations on the liberal–democratic theme.

The representative principle is taken to an extreme in the United States where officials, ranging from the local coroner to the President, are elected by the voters. Many official positions which are filled by appointment in Britain, are open to election in America. In general, US congressmen are less dependent upon a national party machine for their electoral success than their British counterparts in the House of Commons. This, it is claimed, enables them to be more responsive to the wishes of their constituents compared with the party-controlled British MPs.

Although this leads one to the conclusion that in some important respects the American system is more representative than the British, there is another side to the coin. For example the American Cabinet is composed of presidential appointees who are, of course, not elected. Granted, it does not have the power afforded to the British cabinet, but then nor is it bound by a convention of collective cabinet responsibility.

However the notions of representation and responsibility become institutionalized within a political system, it is clear that they not only protect the rights of the governed but also provide greater stability for those who govern. If power in its most positive sense is the ability to get things done, then those in government are more likely to achieve their goals if they and their policies have the people's approval. In a similar way, a system of representative and responsible government is likely to foster a greater willingness on the part of the majority of people to proceed according to established and peaceful patterns of change. Even during testing times of economic and social difficulty a government is better able to maintain law and order if the people know they have access to, and ultimate power over, their leaders.

Essay questions

1 How far does present-day practice conform to the theory of the collective responsibility of the Cabinet? (Oxford, Summer 1982)

2 Should a back-bench MP listen more to his or her party, his or her constituents, or his or her own common sense? (Oxford, Summer 1982)

3 Is British government sufficiently responsive to public opinion? (Oxford, Summer 1984)

4 'MPs are accountable to the national interest and their conscience, hence they are accountable to no-one'. Discuss. (Cambridge, Summer 1984)

5 Whom should an MP obey? His Parliamentary Whips? His constituents? His party conference? His conscience? (London, June 1981)

6 Should MPs rebel, abstain and cross-vote more than they do? Why don't they? (London, January 1982)

7 'Parliament is now failing the nation.' Discuss. (London, June 1983)

8 To what extent is the sponsorship of parliamentary
   candidates consistent with the MP's role as a representative?
   (AEB 1986)

Short-answer questions

1 Distinguish between 'responsible' and 'representative'
   government. (London, June 1979)
2 Distinguish between ministerial and collective responsibility. (London, June 1981)
3 What benefits are supposed to derive from collective
   Cabinet responsibility? (London, June 1983)
4 What is meant when it is said that an MP is a representative
   and not a delegate? (London, June 1983)
5 What are the main features of Burke's theory of the role of
   an MP? (London, January 1984)
6 What is meant by representative government? (London,
   June 1984)
7 Define the concept of electoral mandate. (London,
   January 1985)
8 What is meant by collective responsibility? (London,
   January 1986)
9 Distinguish between a delegate and a representative.
   (London, June 1986)

7 Natural and civil rights

One of the most controversial and elusive concepts which is basic to most political systems is that of human rights. From the outset it is important to identify the close link between the concepts of **freedom** and **rights** and to define the nature of this relationship. One usual interpretation of freedom rests on the notion of an unrestricted existence: an individual is not subject to any unsolicited external pressures to act in a certain way. In this sense one is speaking of freedom from external directives upon one's behaviour, which allows a person to remain passive or to act in response to self-will. An extension of this view which stresses freedom to act in a self-willed way, involves an element of *choice*. Indeed, range of choice features in the measurement of freedom. One box of cornflakes on the breakfast table gives one the choice between a bowl of cornflakes or nothing. A range of cereals increases the possibilities and thereby extends the boundaries of freedom.

Before moving on to consider the nature of the interrelationship between freedom and rights, it is necessary to provide a working definition of the latter. Rights, then, are entitlements. Identifying natural rights has been a centre of debate for philosphers throughout the centuries, that is, whether or not there are entitlements associated with being human, and if so, what are they? Most people agree that there are *natural*, or as they are sometimes described *inalienable rights* and that these can be distinguished from *legal rights* allowed to the citizens by the governments of different nation–states. The constitutions of many states contain natural rights which then become items of law. Many *legal* and *political rights* are based upon *natural rights*. This is certainly the case in liberal democracies: the British model will be examined more closely later in the chapter.

What, then, are these basic rights which human beings

should expect for themselves? The English philosopher John Locke (1632–1704) identified 'life, liberty and property' and the American politician Thomas Jefferson (1743–1826) wrote of 'life, liberty and the pursuit of happiness'. Thomas Hobbes (1588–1679) holds out only two absolute rights: to defend oneself by all means and to seek peace and preserve it. Article 3 of the Universal Declaration of Human Rights, to be found at the end of this chapter, states 'Everyone has the right to life, liberty and security of person.' This Declaration was adopted by the General Assembly of the United Nations (UN) in December 1948, and it called upon all member countries to publicize the text of the Declaration and:

to cause it to be disseminated, displayed, read and expounded principally in schools and other educational institutions, without distinction based on the political status of countries and territories.

The Declaration is worth closer examination for it does provide an international code of individual human rights. It comprises thirty Articles which extend to individual human beings' entitlements, for example:

Article 10:
Everyone is entitled in full equality to a fair and public hearing by an independent and impartial tribunal, in the determination of his rights and obligations and of any criminal charge against him; freedoms from unwanted external controls.

Article 4:
No one shall be held in slavery or servitude; slavery and the slave trade shall be prohibited in all their forms; and freedoms to act in a self-willed way.

Article 13:
Everyone has the right to freedom of movement and residence within the borders of each state.

There is an important dimension which is connected to the notion of rights and that is the notion of *obligations*. These relate to all humans who live in communities and enjoy certain rights. When rights are *universalized*, that is, they relate to everybody, by the same token they apply constraints upon everybody. Article 3, mentioned above, not only extends the right to life, liberty and security of person but also obliges those same individuals *not* to deprive others of these rights. Moreover, Article 1 of the Declaration restrains freedom of action by placing a moral directive upon everybody:

All human beings are born free and equal in dignity and rights. They are endowed with reason and conscience and should act towards one another in a spirit of brotherhood.

National governments may or may not abide by internationally accepted human rights even though these may be enshrined in their constitutions. Certainly governments always preserve for themselves the authority to withdraw rights both natural and legal, if, in their view, circumstances make it necessary to do so.

Rights conferred by membership of society

Certain rights that we possess come not from our status as human beings, but from the fact that we are members of a particular society. These rights are set by a society and outline the extent of individual freedom which will exist within that society. Such rights vary greatly in nature and type from society to society. Rights such as these are best seen, as Professor Crick puts it, as 'things that the law allows us to enjoy . . . or commands others to provide for us: such legal rights are beyond number.' Two important features of such rights is their diversity and that they are capable of being modified or abolished, if the law changes.

These rights tend to be of two sorts: those which enable an individual to carry out certain actions which enable him to be politically effective, for example, the right to free assembly and free speech. The second type of right is to be free from some action which could affect the individual; most western societies consider that the right to be free from arbitrary arrest and imprisonment is an important right. Such rights give a pattern of order and predictability to the life of an individual and thus aid social stability. Perhaps the right to a stable and peaceful existence is one which is of greatest importance, though one which is missing from many societies.

The basic aim of all societies must be to continue in existence over a long period of time. To enable this to happen order is necessary; such order is largely created by the legal and constitutional framework of particular societies. Constitutions often outline the rights that citizens may enjoy: many of these are rights which can be seen as natural rights, others as civil or political rights. One of the clearest expositions of individual rights is contained within the United States Constitution and its Bill of Rights of 1791. This outlines constitutionally guaranteed basic rights which include:

(*a*) The right to a free press, freedom of speech and freedom of assembly (Amendment 1)

(*b*) The right to keep and bear arms (2)

(*c*) The right to be secure against unreasonable search and seizure (4)

(*d*) The right to a speedy and public trial by an impartial jury (6)

(*e*) The right not to be subject to cruel and unusual punishment (8)

(*f*) The right to vote regardless of colour (15) or sex (19). (These last are more recent amendments.)

Exercise
Which of the six rights listed above are 'freedom to do' rights, and which are 'freedom from' rights? Which are natural rights and which are legal or political rights peculiar to the US?

The US Constitution attempts in these elements, and others, to enumerate the rights which are considered essential if the legal and political life of the country is to function effectively. Despite the provision of a constitution there are often times when the rights guaranteed by a constitution are not enforced; thus the fifteenth amendment, passed in 1870, states:

Section 1
The right of citizens of the United States to vote shall not be denied or abridged by the United States or by any State on account of race, colour, or previous condition of servitude.

In reality the right was limited by the actions of the white majority in some states and it was not until the Civil Rights Movement of the 1960s that the reality of blacks enjoying equal voting rights was achieved. A theoretical right is of little use unless that right can be taken for granted.

All societies accept that at some times it is imperative to restrict or suspend some of the rights that have been given to the individual or group. Most commonly such times are during war, national emergency or, increasingly, terrorist activity. The rights that are restricted may include those which the UN

Declaration regards as basic human rights, as well as those rights which are the product of the political culture of a society. The justification for such a suspension of rights hinges upon the need for exceptional action at times of exceptional need; in some circumstances it is necessary to protect the nation by drastic actions. Individual and group rights must be limited for a time for the greater good of the nation. Difficulties arise when the phrase 'the greater good of the nation' becomes equated with what is politically expedient at the time. When the South African government declared a state of emergency in 1986 and imposed censorship on the media, the justification it gave was that outlined above. Most outside observers, however, thought that this action was in reality a way of keeping the black majority of population under the control of a white minority. The 'greater good of the nation' effectively meant what was good for the government.

It must be stressed here that the Western nations are by no means free of such limitations on rights and it is worth remembering that in 1985, Amnesty International claimed that 120 countries were involved in violating human rights, including the UK, the USA, West Germany, France, and even Switzerland.

The great danger is that the rulers of many societies appear to restrict or abolish rights almost at will to suit political expediency. The constitution of the USSR, for instance, is a document which gives many freedoms to its citizens, including freedom of speech, movement, assembly and religion, but it is clear that many of those rights are limited on an almost permanent basis. The justification for this is that it is necessary to restrict such rights in order to protect against counter-revolutionary tendencies.

Groups which seek to extend rights and to inform people of their rights are often subject to harassment because of their actions. The Charter 77 group in Czechoslovakia was set up to monitor the way that the Czech government fulfilled its commitment to protect human and political rights according to the Helsinki Agreement; some of its members have been jailed for their actions. In 1979 there was a great international outcry when members of the group were given harsh jail sentences for carrying on their work. The group remains under pressure.

Although most societies do have a constitution which in theory contains an outline of the rights of citizens, some consistently ignore such constitutions to such a degree as to make the life of the citizens almost completely unpredictable. Rights are ignored at will, arrests and executions are carried out without due process of law and torture is used in a routine way. The former regimes of Idi Amin in Uganda (and indeed the regime of Milton Obote in the same country), Bokassa in the Central African Republic and Duvalier in Haiti, all fall into this category. With almost all rights ignored all of these countries descended into chaos and appalling barbarism. Such regimes perhaps indicate that without some minimum level of political rights a society becomes unstable and may ultimately collapse.

One major difficulty which states face is in reconciling the needs of the majority (however this may be defined), with allowing minorities their rights. The theory of democracy seems to carry the implication that the majority view should dominate but at the same time minority rights should not be ignored. The next chapter will discuss the nature of democracy, but one may surmise that a fair indication of how democratic a country is can be gauged by how readily it is prepared to restrict the rights of its citizens.

Discussion point
Who has the ability to restrict rights? How can citizens have a guarantee that their rights will be upheld?

If citizens have political rights then it is probably also true that governments have rights. Legitimate government has the right to expect respect and compliance from most of its citizens most of the time. To have political rights implies the existence of obligations or duties which the citizen should carry out if he is to be counted as a full member of society. Respect for the law and involvement, however slight, in the political process may be adjudged to be two of the more important duties of a citizen. What is not clear, though, is how far duty should come before individual rights. Some societies have a tradition of individualism: the belief that individual differences should be cultivated and encouraged and that the individual's rights are of paramount importance. Western liberal democracies stress rights and freedoms rather than obligations and duties. In such societies competition is often held in higher regard than co-operation and service. Other societies, for instance those of the Far East, have less of a tradition of individualism and stress the duties rather than the freedoms of an individual. Cultural traditions often bind the individual to duties in relation to larger groups. For the Asian there are important duties to perform in honour of family ancestors as well as those still living. If the individual is not as important as these wider considerations, rights become less important than duties.

Rights in Britain

In the UK great stress is laid on the legal and political rights enjoyed by the population. No government willingly restricts these rights as it realizes that the outcry when such rights are restricted can be very great, unless there is general agreement that an extreme situation is in existence. The lack of a written constitution somewhat complicates matters for it is not always clear what the rights of the individual or group are. The flexibility of the constitution, coupled with an expansion in government action has led many people to the conclusion that rights are under threat in Britain. If government action is increasing the threat that basic rights are being abridged then, the argument goes, we need a Bill of Rights similar to that of the United States. Few people suggest that governments are deliberately limiting rights, but it is suggested that increased volume of legislation, growing bureaucracy and the evolution of government all contribute towards a weakening of the position of the individual in relation to the state.

Many of the rights contained in the US Bill of Rights are considered to be essential in the UK – the right to free assembly, freedom of speech and freedom of religious belief, for example. Whereas the US Bill of Rights can only be changed by a complex constitutional procedure, the same is not true in Britain. Parliament has absolute power to make or unmake any law. This gives parliament, or more particularly the government, ability in theory to withdraw rights, or give rights, almost at will. In practice this is clearly not so, for the citizen is protected from great changes by the democratic political system of Britain. The government realizes that if it is

to be re-elected it must not alienate too many individuals by
its actions. Her Majesty's Opposition, if it is doing its job
correctly, is one means of checking arbitrary government
action. One course which is not open to the citizen is to
question the legality of an Act of Parliament, except in one of
the international courts. No court in Britain can do other than
interpret the law – it cannot judge as to whether the law is good
or bad. Clearly, though, a government may not act outside its
legal rights and if it does it may well face a law suit.

Rights exist on a number of levels in Britain; from the highly
specific to the highly general. Some of the many general rights
have evolved as our society has evolved over the centuries
and, as with specific rights, will continue to alter. We now
consider the right to a good education to be essential for all
children, yet a little over a hundred years ago this was seen as
neither possible, nor desirable. Governments, since the
Second World War, have accepted that all people should have
the right to employment and have worked towards creating a
full-employment economy. This last example may illustrate
the way in which these rights change – it appears that the 'right
to work' is not an absolute right as recent governments have
followed policies which have deliberately created unemployment in pursuance of a healthier economy. One difficulty with
highly generalized rights is to discern whether there is an
instance within them of irreducible rights. Thus the individual
may have the general right to engage in political activity,
though this can be restricted under certain circumstances,
but is the right to vote (which is part of the general right to
engage in political activity) sacrosanct?

Discussion point
Can you foresee any situation in which the right to vote could
be withdrawn? Would such action ever be justified?

Many politicians, for instance Lord Hailsham, have argued
that there are certain rights which should never be abridged,
but that at present the individual has no guarantee that they
will not be. Growth of legislation which affects the individual,
growth of group activity and the overall weakening of this
position of the individual within the political system means,
they argue, that a Bill of Rights is essential in the United

Kingdom. These developments are taking place but to adopt the Bill of Rights solution would mean a break with tradition and the adoption of a written constitution which could restrict the flexibility which is such a useful part of the constitutional framework.

Governments in the UK do not seem to be engaged in systematic and widespread action to limit individual rights but there are times when even our most cherished rights are abridged. The liberty of an individual is safeguarded in a number of ways under normal circumstances. Anyone arrested on a criminal charge must be told immediately the reason for his arrest and be brought speedily before a court. Wherever possible a defendant should be brought to court within twenty-four hours. If this is not possible then a police officer must release the defendant on bail by discharging him temporarily and ordering him to appear in court at an appointed time. This is the usual situation when the offence is not serious. The court may also grant bail. Anyone who believes himself to be detained unlawfully may secure release through a writ of *habeas corpus* served on the person detaining him. In accordance with such a writ a person who detains another must appear in court to show the reason for the detention. If no lawful reason is established then the prisoner must be released. This right is of fundamental importance in the British system, for it protects the individual from the power of state.

At times, though, even this right has to be suspended as in the case of Northern Ireland. Ulster has been the one part of the UK, over the past ten years, where many basic rights have been withdrawn. The activities of the IRA and other para-military organizations have led to the suspension of the government in Stormont, troops being used as security forces, detention without trial (though this no longer occurs) and, on occasions, the use of torture to extract information. The Prevention of Terrorism Act 1976 allows the police to arrest and hold suspects without charge for up to forty-eight hours. This can be extended by a further five days with the Home Secretary's approval. The pamphlet, *Human Rights in the United Kingdom*, describes the situation as follows:

In Northern Ireland itself emergency powers have been necessary to combat terrorism. These include the power to stop, search, arrest

and question people on suspicion, the proscribing of organisations:
and the abolition of trial by jury for terrorist offences.

Certainly the official view is clear that the circumstances in
Northern Ireland were such that this type of emergency action
(or something similar) was needed, but it does show that at
certain times even basic rights are abolished in the UK. If such
actions are justified in the case of Northern Ireland to
preserve a semblance of order, would similar action be
justified in the case of a strike which was crippling the country,
or to control a potentially disruptive political party?

The pamphlet previously mentioned, which gives the
official view, claims that rights are sufficiently protected by
our present political system and that there are many legal and
non-legal restraints on the abuse of governmental power.

There are vital non-legal safeguards against the abuse of governmental power; these include unwritten parliamentary conventions,
the sense of 'fair play' of legislators and administrations, the
vigilance of the parliamentary opposition parties and of individual
Members of Parliament, the influence of a free Press and public
opinion, and the right to change the Government through free
elections with a secret ballot.

While it is clear that circumstances may arise which lead to
the restriction of rights this restriction is not without its own
dangers, despite the optimistic view stated above. Once it has
been accepted that rights should be taken away it is often then
very difficult to have them reinstated. Natural caution
concerning a re-occurrence of the circumstances which lead to
the suspension of rights, the inbuilt conservatism of many
political systems, or a realization that life is simpler for those
in power if certain rights no longer exist, may all help to
persuade politicians that the reinstatement of rights should be
deferred. The continuation of the Prevention of Terrorism Act
into its second decade is justified by the government on the
grounds of continuing need, but opponents claim that the
need for this temporary measure no longer exists. It is
tempting to argue that while there is a terrorist threat such
legislation is necessary, but it can also be argued that the long-
term cost of the legislation in lessening rights is too great a
price to pay.

One trend in the UK in recent years has been the growth of legislation to ensure that certain sections of the population are able to rely on the force of law to gain their rights. The Sex Discrimination Act 1975, and the Equal Pay Act 1970, combined, give women greater protection than ever before. It is now unlawful to discriminate against a person, or to give lower pay, on the basis of sex. In a similar vein there have been a number of Race Relations Acts (1965, 1968 and 1976) which have attempted to improve the position of ethnic minorities by protecting them from discrimination. This type of legislation illustrates a difficulty; to enable these groups to enjoy fairer treatment has meant that some rights of others have had to be limited. In order to improve the employment position of women, it was necessary to limit the right of employers to decide who they wanted to employ. There are now certain reasons which are not acceptable as justifications for refusing someone a job. Clearly giving more rights to women has been at the expense of limiting rights of employers. There may be conflict between the rights of various individuals but increasingly there seems to be conflict between the rights of the individual and the rights of groups, especially the government.

It has already been noted that government activity is increasingly affecting the individual, but it should also be clear that a government has the right to act in this way. It is elected to govern and in order to do so it may have to change or amend the rights that are given to citizens. The right to govern can often be seen to be in conflict with the rights of the individual; the Prevention of Terrorism Act, previously mentioned, whilst limiting individual rights, was justified as being the only way to protect individual life and to enable government to continue. In a society where Parliament has the ability to make or unmake any law it would be said that government has to have the right to act as it sees fit. Such an argument can be dangerous as it implies that all government restrictions on rights are justified if the government say they are. There has been a growth in individual and group complaints on questions of maladministration. To deal with such complaints, quasi-legal machinery has grown since the Second World War. This includes tribunals, public inquiries and an official who receives such complaints – the Ombudsman. A parallel local system has also recently developed.

Greater attention has been focused on group rights in recent years. Interest-group activity has become more and more common and effective and some such groups now have rights which the ordinary citizen does not have. Major interest groups, as we have seen, claim the right to be consulted by government on matters which affect them and to influence policy formulation. Such access and influence are effectively denied to the individual unless he is prepared to participate in such group activity.

In the industrial field, it has been argued that group power has now reached the stage where individual rights are ignored. Article 23 of the Universal Declaration of Human Rights, says that everyone has the right 'to free choice of employment', but clearly this has not been strictly true in Britain. In certain industries the right to employment has traditionally been dependent on union membership, that is, the 'closed shop'. Without such membership an individual could not be employed. When industrial action is taken it often affects other individuals or groups; so-called secondary action can lead to people not directly involved in a dispute being harmed by the dispute. The conclusion of the 1979 Conservative Government was that these situations imposed an unwarranted restriction on individual rights by groups. As a result they introduced several pieces of legislation to alter the balance. It would be easy to fall into the trap of thinking that unions are harmful organizations, but clearly this is too simple an approach. The right to belong to a union is a basic right in Britain. It enables the individual to gain by negotiations carried out for him by trained personnel – individuals may be unaware of their rights or be unable to exercise them effectively, but by joining together with others, they may be able to realize their rights.

A Bill of Rights for Britain

The many issues surrounding human rights, how to define them and how they are to be preserved, come into play in the debate on whether or not Britain should have a codified set of principles which protect minority and individual rights. Arguments on both sides are directly associated with the broader question of whether Britain should have a written constitution. It is not the direct concern of this book to explore in detail this major area of contention, but it would be illuminating, in view of the foregoing analysis of natural and civil rights, to outline some of the main arguments for and against a Bill of Rights.

Those who support such a move, do so because they believe Britain is over-governed with too much power in too few hands. Once elected, the British cabinet with its permanent Civil Service advisers is in a virtually unassailable position. Lord Hailsham has described this situation as an 'elective dictatorship'. The function of the powers of the executive and legislature in a cabinet of twenty people or so endangers both individual and minority rights which have been so painstakingly won and preserved over the centuries. It is claimed that the checks installed in the system to counter executive powers are no longer adequate for the task, particularly in relation to the development of strong, disciplined political parties. Those who wish to strengthen individual and minority rights, *vis-à-vis* growing state power, support a Bill of Rights of some kind to help achieve this.

The case for a Bill of Rights
1   A Bill of Rights would clarify the areas of control by government, and the rights of the citizen. There would come into being an agreed set of basic principles against which government actions could be measured, and if found wanting could be called before a constitutional court for judgment. In a democracy, parliament itself should be entirely subject to the rule of law. Moreover, the inadequacies of the English courts could be remedied – for example, their inability to uphold the rights of privacy in relation to telephone tapping.

2   Britain is not only a signatory to the UN Declaration on Human Rights, but also a party to the European Convention on Human Rights. A British citizen, therefore, has access to the European Court at Strasbourg if he feels a basic democratic right has been violated. However, a major criticism is that redress of a grievance through this channel is slow and laborious, often taking a number of years. British governments are already bound by international law in this way; what is desired is that the means of redressing grievances be brought closer to home, made more accessible and speedy.

3   Within the American experience there are illustrations of
the Supreme Court acting as the guardian of the US
Constitution, coming down in favour of the individual or
minority group against the State. In the Brown *v* Board of
Education Case (1954), the Supreme Court ruled that racial
segregation of black children in schools was inherently
unequal and therefore unconstitutional. Although the segregation issue caused racial strife in the years that followed, the
final result was the Civil Rights Acts of 1964. In this way, the
US Supreme Court ruling was a major factor in gaining equal
opportunity for the minority black community.

4   There is an educational advantage to be gained from
having a clear statement of basic rights. A statement of this
kind would create a more widespread understanding of basic
principles. In the United States every student is taught the
first ten amendments which comprise the US Bill of Rights.

The case against a Bill of Rights
1   There are always problems involved in the preservation of
individual and minority rights. The question is whether a Bill
of Rights would help or hinder the solutions to these
problems. Within the British constitutional tradition the
argument for parliamentary sovereignty is a crucial one. MPs
are forced to remain sensitive and responsive to the wishes of
the electorate in order to have a chance of securing a fresh
mandate at a future election. This relationship with people
provides the basis for the authority and power of parliament to
legislate on all matters including individual and minority
rights. The introduction of a written constitution, including a
Bill of Rights, would mean that on many crucial issues of
contention the final decision would be taken from the elected
assembly of representatives and placed in the hands of
unelected, unaccountable judges sitting in a constitutional
court – the very judges who are often criticized for being out of
touch with the lives of ordinary people. Inevitably power
would shift from the people's representatives to the judges.

2   However beneficial a Bill of Rights has been in the United
States this in itself is no argument for introducing the same in
Britain. There are different historical and cultural traditions
to take into account. Furthermore, judges have protected

rights to a considerable extent, for example in the Tameside case, previously mentioned. Civil liberties are protected by a legal system which carries safeguards including the right to take questionable decisions by juries to the Court of Appeal where they may be over-ruled. In the same vein, no confession is permissible unless it is freely given. Even if rights needed further protection, there is no evidence that a Bill of Rights would serve that pupose. There is no marked contrast between the number of times Britain is called to account before the Strasbourg Court and those of other countries with written constitutions and bills of rights. In addition to the protection of rights afforded by the British system, European Court rulings have exerted moral pressure on governments to cease certain activities such as the banning of certain interrogation methods in Northern Ireland.

3   The whole question of which rights should be selected for inclusion in a Bill of Rights, requires examination. Are they to be general principles such as freedom of speech, assembly and association, or specific principles, such as the right not to belong to a closed shop? If it was to be a set of general principles then it would be so vague that judges would have complete power to interpret what the provisions meant and parliament would be unable to challenge them. If it was to be a specific set of rights then future parliaments would be bound to those decisions made by the parliament involved at the point when the Bill of Rights was formulated. This could have meant the outlawing of the closed shop during the Conservative Government 1970–4, or the entrenching of it in the Labour Government 1974–9. Either way, subsequent parliamentary majorities would find it difficult to overrule what might have been included in a Bill of Rights at either time.

4   Such a situation would cut across the doctrine of the sovereignty of parliament and create a political role for the appointed guardians of the constitution. Even if it was concluded that the increased powers of the British executive were anti-democratic, the answer ought to be sought in strengthening traditional checks and balances or devising new ones. Perhaps committees of back-bench MPs should have their investigative powers increased, the public given more

access to government information through a Freedom of
Information Act, and the operation of the Official Secrets Act
reviewed. Whatever innovative measures might be taken, the
option of a written constitution with a Bill of Rights would
cost too highly in terms of the loss of a sovereign parliament's
freedom and flexibility to respond to new situations as they arise.

Universal Declaration of Human Rights

On 10 December 1948 the General Assembly of the United
Nations adopted and proclaimed the Universal Declaration of
Human Rights, the full text of which appears below. Following
this historical act the Assembly called upon all member
countries to publicize the text of the Declaration and 'to
cause it to be disseminated, displayed, read and expounded
principally in schools and other educational institutions,
without distinction based on the political status of countries
or territories.'

Preamble
Whereas recognition of the inherent dignity and of the equal
and inalienable rights of all members of the human family is
the foundation of freedom, justice and peace in the world,
Whereas disregard and contempt for human rights have
resulted in barbarous acts which have outraged the conscience
of mankind, and the advent of a world in which human beings
shall enjoy freedom of speech and belief and freedom from
fear and want has been proclaimed as the highest aspiration of
the common people,
Whereas it is essential, if man is not to be compelled to have
recourse, as a last resort, to rebellion against tyranny and
oppression, that human rights should be protected by the rule
of law,
Whereas it is essential to promote the development of
friendly relations between nations,
Whereas the peoples of the United Nations have in the
Charter reaffirmed their faith in fundamental human rights, in
the dignity and worth of the human person and in the equal
rights of men and women and have determined to promote
social progress and better standards of life in larger freedom,
Whereas Member States have pledged themselves to

achieve, in co-operation with the United Nations, the promotion of universal respect for and observance of human rights and fundamental freedoms,

Whereas a common understanding of these rights and freedoms is of the greatest importance for the full realization of this pledge,

Now, therefore, The General Assembly proclaims
This Universal Declaration of Human Rights as a common standard of achievement for all peoples and all nations, to the end that every individual and every organ of society, keeping this Declaration constantly in mind, shall strive by teaching and education to promote respect for these rights and freedoms and by progressive measures, national and international, to secure their universal and effective recognition and observance, both among the peoples of Member States themselves and among the peoples of territories under their jurisdiction.

Article 1 All human beings are born free and equal in dignity and rights. They are endowed with reason and conscience and should act towards one another in a spirit of brotherhood.

Article 2 Everyone is entitled to all the rights and freedoms set forth in this Declaration, without distinction of any kind, such as race, colour, sex, language, religion, political or other opinion, national or social origin, property, birth or other status.

Furthermore, no distinction shall be made on the basis of the political, jurisdictional or international status of the country or territory to which a person belongs, whether it be independent, trust, non-self-governing or under any other limitation of sovereignty.

Article 3 Everyone has the right to life, liberty and security of person.

Article 4 No one shall be held in slavery or servitude; slavery and the slave trade shall be prohibited in all their forms.

Article 5 No one shall be subjected to torture or to cruel, inhuman or degrading treatment or punishment.

Article 6 Everyone has the right to recognition everywhere as a person before the law.

Article 7 All are equal before the law and are entitled without any discrimination to equal protection from the law. All are entitled to equal protection against any discrimination in violation of this Declaration and against any incitement to such discrimination.

Article 8   Everyone has the right to an effective remedy by the competent national tribunals for acts violating the fundamental rights granted him by the constitution or by law.

Article 9   No one shall be subjected to arbitrary arrest, detention or exile.

Article 10   Everyone is entitled in full equality to a fair and public hearing by an independent and impartial tribunal, in the determination of his rights and obligations and of any criminal charge against him.

Article 11   (1) Everyone charged with a penal offence has the right to be presumed innocent until proved guilty according to law in a public trial at which he has had all the guarantees necessary for his defence.

(2) No one shall be held guilty of any penal offence on account of any act or omission which did not constitute a penal offence, under national or international law, at the time when it was committed. Nor shall a heavier penalty be imposed than the one that was applicable at the time the penal offence was committed.

Article 12   No one shall be subjected to arbitrary interference with his privacy, family, home or correspondence, nor to attacks upon his honour and reputation. Everyone has the right to the protection of the law against such interference or attacks.

Article 13   (1) Everyone has the right to freedom of movement and residence within the borders of each state.

(2) Everyone has the right to leave any country, including his own, and to return to his country.

Article 14   (1) Everyone has the right to seek and to enjoy in other countries asylum from persecution.

(2) This right may not be invoked in the case of prosecutions genuinely arising from non-political crimes or from acts contrary to the purposes and principles of the United Nations.

Article 15   (1) Everyone has the right to a nationality.

(2) No one shall be arbitrarily deprived of his nationality nor denied the right to change his nationality.

Article 16   (1) Men and women of full age, without any limitation due to race, nationality or religion, have the right to marry and to found a family. They are entitled to equal rights as to marriage, during marriage and at its dissolution.

(2) Marriage shall be entered into only with the free and full consent of the intending spouses.

(3) The family is the natural and fundamental group unit of society and is entitled to protection by society and the state.

Article 17 (1) Everyone has the right to own property alone as well as in association with others.

(2) No one shall be arbitrarily deprived of his property.

Article 18 Everyone has the right to freedom of thought, conscience and religion; this right includes freedom to change his religion or belief, and freedom either alone or in community with others and in public or private, to manifest his religion or belief in teaching, practice, worship and observance.

Article 19 Everyone has the right to freedom of opinion and expression; this right includes freedom to hold opinions without interference and to seek, receive and impart information and ideas through any media and regardless of frontiers.

Article 20 (1) Everyone has the right to freedom of peaceful assembly and association.

(2) No one may be compelled to belong to an association.

Article 21 (1) Everyone has the right to take part in the government of his country, directly or through freely chosen representatives.

(2) Everyone has the right of equal access to public service in his country.

(3) The will of the people shall be the basis of the authority of government; this will shall be expressed in periodic and genuine elections which shall be by universal and equal suffrage and shall be held by secret vote or by equivalent free voting procedures.

Article 22 Everyone, as a member of society, has the right to social security and is entitled to realization, through national effort and international co-operation and in accordance with the organization and resources of each state, of the economic, social and cultural rights indispensable for his dignity and the free development of his personality.

Article 23 (1) Everyone has the right to work, to free choice of employment, to just and favourable conditions of work and to protection against unemployment.

(2) Everyone, without any discrimination, has the right to

equal pay for equal work.

(3) Everyone who works has the right to just and favourable remuneration ensuring for himself and his family an existence worthy of human dignity, and supplemented, if necessary, by other means of social protection.

(4) Everyone has the right to form and to join trade unions for the protection of his interests.

Article 24 Everyone has the right to rest and leisure, including reasonable limitation of working hours and periodic holidays with pay.

Article 25 (1) Everyone has the right to a standard of living adequate for the health and well-being of himself and of his family, including food, clothing, housing and medical care and necessary social services, and the right to security in the event of unemployment, sickness, disability, widowhood, old age or other lack of livelihood in circumstances beyond his control.

(2) Motherhood and childhood are entitled to special care and assistance. All children, whether born in or out of wedlock, shall enjoy the same social protection.

Article 26 (1) Everyone has the right to education. Education shall be free, at least in the elementary and fundamental stages. Elementary education shall be compulsory. Technical and professional education shall be made generally available and higher education shall be equally accessible to all on the basis of merit.

(2) Education shall be directed to the full development of the human personality and to the strengthening of respect for human rights and fundamental freedoms. It shall promote understanding, tolerance and friendship among all nations, racial or religious groups, and shall further the activities of the United Nations for the maintenance of peace.

(3) Parents have a prior right to choose the kind of education that shall be given to their children.

Article 27 (1) Everyone has the right freely to participate in the cultural life of the community, to enjoy the arts and to share in scientific advancement and its benefits.

(2) Everyone has the right to the protection of the moral and material interests resulting from any scientific, literary or artistic production of which he is the author.

Article 28 Everyone is entitled to a social and international order in which the rights and freedoms set forth in this Declaration can be fully realized.

Article 29 (1) Everyone has duties to the community in which alone the free and full development of his personality is possible.

(2) In the exercise of his rights and freedoms, everyone shall be subject only to such limitations as are determined by law solely for the purpose of securing due recognition and respect for the rights and freedoms of others and of meeting the just requirements of morality, public order and the general welfare in a democratic society.

(3) These rights and freedoms may in no case be exercised contrary to the purposes and principles of the United Nations.

Article 30 Nothing in this Declaration may be interpreted as implying for any state, group or person any right to engage in any activity or to perform any act aimed at the destruction of any of the rights and freedoms set forth herein.

Essay questions

1 'Since the Constitution of Great Britain is "unwritten" there is no special protection for "fundamental rights".' Should there be? What problems are likely to arise in attempting to provide a new 'Bill of Rights'? (JMB, June 1977)

2 To what extend should the citizens of any one country (such as Britain) concern themselves with 'human rights' in any other country? (Oxford, Summer 1983)

3 The advantages and disadvantages of a Bill of Rights have often been discussed in Britain. Which rights, if any, do you think should be entrenched in the British Constitution? Give reasons for your answer. (Cambridge, Summer 1983)

4 What are the principal threats to citizens' rights in Britain today, and how might such rights be protected? (Cambridge, Summer 1984)

5 What limitations do you think there should be on freedom of speech? (London, January 1979)

6 How are the rights of citizens defended in Britain? What improvements could be made? (London, January 1984)

7 Britain is one of the few countries of the West whose citizens are not protected by a Bill of Rights. Why do you think this is so? (London, June 1984)

8   Proposals for a Bill of Rights are most often made when
     Labour Governments are in power. Why is this so?
     (London, January 1986)

Short-answer questions

1   Distinguish between civil rights and natural rights. (London,
     June 1979)
2   Distinguish between individual and collective rights.
     (London, January 1981)
3   What sort of duties, as opposed to rights, do citizens have?
     (London, January 1984)
4   What are the differences between a Liberal's and a
     Socialist's views on basic human rights? (London, June
     1985)
5   Define the concept of civil rights. (London, January 1986)
6   What are the duties of a citizen? (London, June 1986)

8 Democracy

In this final chapter we turn to a consideration of democracy, a complex concept which involves an understanding of all the concepts hitherto considered. The main aim is to show that democracy may exist in more than one form and that all societies, including Britain, have some flaws in their claims to being democratic. Many people in the *liberal* **democracies** often discount the claim of other societies to being democracies because their systems seem so dissimilar to those of Western liberal democracies – many societies have elements of democratic government, some of which we are unwilling to see. Equally, Britain has elements within its political system which some observers may consider to be less than democratic.

Most countries claim that they are democracies, countries as diverse as Great Britain, China, USA, the USSR, India and Singapore. If one wants to describe democracy it is not sufficient merely to ask whether a country calls itself a democracy, for at the moment democracy is a 'fashionable' and 'good' form of government, and many countries would be unwilling to describe themselves as being anything other than democratic. What is needed is some idea of the types of democracy to be found and what characteristics, if any, they share.

Historical development

Democracy as an idea has its roots in ancient Greece, notably Athens; democracy was the form of government in which all qualified citizens were allowed and even required, to participate in the government of the city-state. The word democratic is derived from two Greek words which can be translated as 'people power'. This 'direct' form of democracy has been taken to be the purest form of democracy but even in Greece there were limits to who was classified as a 'qualified citizen'. Among those excluded were slaves, women and children. The main feature of 'direct' democracy was participation, the citizen was expected to play a positive role in controlling his own life rather than delegating the task of ruling to somebody else.

With the decline of the Greeks the notion of democracy also underwent a decline, for in most countries the natural form of government was seen to be that of the rule of the few over the many. This was exemplified by Europe up to the nineteenth century – most countries were ruled by monarchs or by the nobility. The bulk of the population was excluded from self-rule as they were not thought to be capable of making the necessary decisions for themselves. The idea that the skill to govern rests upon education and upbringing meant that those who lacked such a background were thought incapable of making good decisions. Democracy was associated with rule by the mass of illiterate peasants; it was a dangerous form of government because those able to rule – the nobility – would be under the control of the masses. It was not believed that the majority were capable of governing. Indeed, after the French Revolution in 1789 and the excesses of the 'Terror' which followed, fear of 'mobocracy' and the 'tyranny of the majority' became more apparent in Britain. Many of the early agitations in Britain, for improved conditions were seen as the beginning of a similar revolution.

A variation of the idea of democracy being linked to educational standards is still common, and the belief that many of the underdeveloped nations of the world can never be democratic until the standard of education has been raised to ensure a literate electorate, is also widely held. This theory must be doubted for in practice it seems that countries with low levels of literacy, for instance India, can also become relatively stable democracies.

Democracy in the nineteenth century

It was during the nineteenth century that the notion of democracy came to have two distinct interpretations. In line with the radical tradition, democracy was essentially popular power – rule by the majority. However, a modification evolved in the form of representative democracy which emphasized rule by elected representatives. It was commended by the ruling elite in Britain on the grounds that it maintained continuity and was adaptable to highly populated societies. Orthodox accounts of English history trace the extension of the franchise as the development of liberal democracy in England. It is important at this stage to provide a brief clarification of this process.

The nineteenth century began with Britain at war with France and the events of the French Revolution still fresh in men's minds. The period after 1815 was primarily one of social and economic distress for the masses, a situation exacerbated to the point of disorder by the repressive policies of a self-protective ruling elite. Landowners were the main ruling group whose position rested upon birth, wealth, accumulated governmental 'know-how' and self-preservatory legislation. Democracy, in both senses, was to these men a revolutionary idea which threatened their very existence. Hardly surprising, therefore, that their fears of a repetition of the French experience were translated into savage repression of all manifestations of popular power. Edmund Burke articulated the view in his *Reflections on the Revolution in France* when he condemned what he saw as uncontrolled power which suppressed minorities, most significantly the property-owning minority.

Yet radical thought was having an impact. As the industrialization of Britain progressed the migration from the country-side continued to concentrate people in industrial centres which in turn created a new consciousness of the people's conditions of life and provided a greater potential to improve the conditions. Robert Owen's Grand National Consolidated Trades Union and the Chartist Movement for political reform, were both daring in conception but abortive in effect. These are but a sample of the causes to which support was given and reflect the awakening of new consciousness amongst working people in Britain.

However, the result was not a revolution of the kind which preceded the foundation of people's democracies in twentieth-century Russia and China. From the last Chartist petition in 1848 to the foundation of the Labour Representation Committee in 1900 the working class was not strongly politically minded. Certainly there was no orchestrated demand for a distinct working-class party.

In the first place, working-class support was diverted from political reform after the failure of Chartism and given to other movements such as trades unions, co-operatives and friendly societies, all of which continued to gain strength in pursuit of their objectives and which provided the basis for much interest-group activity in the twentieth century. In the second place, the development of representative democracy was, at least in part, a conscious effort to mitigate what the ruling elite believed to be the excesses of radical democracy. Both the Liberal and Conservative parties offered gradual social and economic reforms which offset any early demands for the creation of a distinct working-class party.

After the first Reform Act of 1832, electoral reform began to strengthen the position of the working class. The Second Reform Act in 1867, carried through under Lord Derby's Conservative Government, gave the vote to male householders in the towns and to the £12 ratepayers in the counties. Consquently, the electorate was almost doubled. Bribery and intimidation at election time were eradicated by the Secret Ballot Act of 1872. In 1884, Gladstone's Liberal Government steered through parliament the Third Reform Act which extended the right to vote to all male householders in the countryside. The working class of town and country now became a majority of the electorate and yet, by and large, for the remainder of the nineteenth century they cast their votes for the Liberal and Conservative parties.

Nevertheless, towards the end of the nineteenth century, socialism was capturing the minds of some men. This doctrine featured community ownership and development of the main sources of national wealth such as coal, mines, railways and evn land, for the benefit of all. It stressed the brotherhood of men and that all men are of equal worth and should be treated with equal respect. Socialists maintained that large inequalities in wealth were wrong and should be eradicated if a fair and just society was to be created. Such ideas were not as alien as they would have been earlier in the century for 'collectivist' laws, such as the Factory Acts and Public Health Acts, which limited private freedom for the good of the community, were already on the statute book.

Influenced by important works such as Karl Marx's *Kapital* published in 1876 and Henry George's *Progress and Poverty* published in 1879, small socialist groups such as the Social Democratic Federation, the Socialist League and the Fabian Society were formed. Eventually the Independent Labour Party was created in 1893 and in 1900 a Labour Representation Committee was formed, committed to the formation of 'A distinct Labour group in parliament'. The Labour Representation Committee, which in 1906 was renamed the Labour Party, soon replaced the Liberals as the main opposition to the Conservatives in the British two-party system. The Labour Party formed its first government in 1924, but it is really in the period since the Second World War that it has competed with the Conservative Party for the title of the 'normal party of government'. In the period 1945–86, Labour was in office for seventeen years and the Conservative Party for twenty-four years. To date, the dominant social democratic element within the Labour Party has upheld representative, parliamentary democracy and worked a mixed economy, that is, one embracing both public and private ownership.

As we have seen, two distinct views of democracy developed in the nineteenth century. The first view of democracy was that held by most of the agitators – they wanted more control over their own destiny. To these men democracy meant being involved in decision-making and in controlling not only their political, but also their working lives. This type of view was reinforced by the extension of education to the working class, which meant that many of the agitators were now literate. The fact that the majority of working people were uneducated and, therefore, unable to make informed decisions had long been an argument against extending democracy.

The second view of democracy was that which came to be supported by the ruling class – democracy was seen as a way of selecting a government. Direct democracy was impossible in a large industrial society, so representative democracy (the people elect representatives to help the governmental process) was the only viable type. Democracy, then, meant extending the range of qualified voters rather than expecting the people to be actively involved in government. Clearly this second view of democracy is *static*, that is, democracy is achieved when people have the vote. The first view is *dynamic* and implies that democracy is an ideal to be aimed for, that we should be constantly looking for ways to improve the system, to give more people an opportunity to participate in government. Undoubtedly it is the second view that has for a long time dominated British political thinking.

Exercise 2
Is direct democracy possible in a modern industrial society or not?

Democratic theory

Although in Britain democratic reforms came to be seen as inevitable and, to most people, to be desirable; in other parts of the world this was not so. A group of writers began to argue that democracy is not possible because government is always in the hands of the few at the top of society – the *Élite*. Because this was so, ordinary people were permanently excluded from government and it follows from this that democracy must be a myth. These *Classical Élitists*, such as Wilfredo Pareto and Gaetano Mosca, while arguing against democratic ideas, paradoxically provided the groundwork for a development of the second view of democracy outlined above, formulating a new theory of democracy which has become extremely influential in the twentieth century.

The *Democratic Élitist* or *Pluralist* conception of democracy, which suggests that democracy is linked to competition between groups and the right to vote, has been especially influential in the USA. Writers such as Kornhauser, Lipset, Schumpeter and C. Wright Mills, have argued that direct democracy has disappeared and can never be re-established in modern industrial societies because of the size and complexity of such societies. Power, then, must be a minority phenomenon – government is always in the hands of a few. The main distinguishing factor of this model of democracy is that government is carried out for the benefit of the majority by representatives chosen by the people. The mainstay of modern democracy is that no group can count on automatic support from the electorate. To gain that support, groups (usually political parties) have to compete against other groups for the elector's vote. This competition ensures that policies will remain moderate (to attract as many votes as possible) and that any group which fails to live up to its promises can expect to be thrown out by the electorate at the next opportunity. This view of democracy also emphasizes the positive role of pressure groups in the democratic process. They are seen as alternative ways for the individual to be represented. J. A. Schumpeter has given a succinct description of this pluralist view of democracy in *Capitalism, Socialism and Democracy*:

The democratic method is the institutional arrangement for arriving at political decisions in which individuals acquire the power to decide by means of a competitive struggle for the people's vote.

So, for the pluralist, democracy becomes primarily an arrangement by which a government is chosen; the electorate are relegated to mere votecasters. Pluralists see that participation is possible through elections and through interest groups. The only alternative to competition between élites is one élite. A *totalitarian* system is one in which the essential elements of democracy are absent, there are no competing parties or interest groups. One élite rules and tries to control all elements of life and the individual is powerless to control such an élite. Countries such as the USSR are totalitarian because of their lack of a competitive political system and their domination by one élite – the Communist Party élite. The pluralists argue that such countries are non-democratic, despite their claims to be 'people's democracies'.

The pluralist view of democracy has been useful because it limits the number of countries that can be considered to be democracies; certainly the USA and Great Britain would qualify as democracies if one accepts the premises of this theory, but few Third World countries and no communist countries would qualify as democracies. One of the major criticisms of this view of democracy is that it describes some features of Western countries, concludes these are democracies, and then taking Western democracy as its model, asserts that any country which does not fit in with this interpretation is not a democracy – seemingly a case of self-justification.

The second strand in democratic ideas, which stresses participation, can be traced back to political philosophers such as Jean Jacques Rousseau, but the practical stand for this type of democracy dates really from the early nineteenth

century and the French Revolution. Before this there had
been attempts to build utopian communities based on
participation but most of these had failed. The view that
people should be involved in controlling their own lives
became a popular one in the nineteenth century, but it was
largely overshadowed by the static view of democracy as being
concerned mainly with extending the franchise to as many as
possible. Participatory democratic theories hold that the vote
is only one aspect of people being able to shape their own lives.
The rise of trade unionism in the nineteenth century can be
seen as part of this same general pattern. This view that
people should participate more actively is a more radical one,
and the major proponent of this type of approach was Karl
Marx. Marx argued that all societies of the past and those of
the present are based on class conflict. He was writing in the
nineteenth century so we do not know what his opinion would
have been of the 'communist' or 'capitalist' countries of today.
According to Marx, government is carried out by one class for
its own, mainly economic, benefit, and not for the benefit of
the mass of the populace. The people in power represent a
definite ruling class, working for their own benefit and against
the interests of the mass of the population. The people who
obtain power in this ruling class are distinguished by their
similar educational and social backgrounds. In such a
situation the fact that ordinary people have the vote does not
matter, as they can only choose between members of the ruling
class and not from their peers. Democracy cannot exist while
one class dominates another both economically and politically. The only way for the mass of the people, and especially
working-class people, to control their own lives is to abolish
the existing class system and the existing society. To do this
would require a revolution after which a 'socialist', and then
a 'communist', society would come into being. In such a
communist society all people would have equal rights and the
ability to develop their potential to the full. Although the
Marxist analysis of present society is not one which is held
by most people in Britain, there are reasons to feel that the
lack of a meaningful political choice in Britain, in terms of
choice between parties, can be interpreted as confirming
Marx's analysis.

Although it is Marxists who have been most critical of the

assumption that because we have universal adult suffrage we have democracy, they are by no means the only group. The Liberal/SDP Alliance have been vociferous in their cries for an end to the two-party system because they feel that such a system ensures that many people never have a government who will listen to, or sympathize with, their views. They feel that other European countries with some type of proportional representation, and often multi-party systems, are more democratic than Britain. Although it is common to explain the Alliance's support for proportional representation in terms of self-interest, it is very clear that they want to make government more responsive to public opinion and less remote from people's lives. In common with Labour politicians they have clled for more open government and less secrecy. The Official Secrets Act is a major target for their concern.

As we have seen, there are two basic views of democracy. The dynamic model sees democracy as being an ideal to aim for. This view implies that we should never be satisfied with our political system but should be looking constantly for ways to improve the system, in order to make it more immediate to as many people as possible. The second, static model, implies that there are some societies which are automatically democracies because they produce their governments in a certain way, by competition between political parties. Taking this definition we can be said to have democracy in Britain. Both views hold elements of the truth and we shall go on to see how they can be applied to Britain, once we have looked at the claims of some other systems to being democratic.

Democracy in the twentieth century

The object of this section is to give perspective to the development of the democratic idea in the twentieth century. Throughout, categorizations will be made which must be seen as drawing broad distinctions rather than providing 'watertight' definitions. We shall be examining more closely the tenets of democracy as applied in First World countries; the tenets of proletarian democracy as applied in Second World countries; and providing a perspective on democracy as a concept in Third World politics. First, however, we must briefly indicate useful ways by which nation-states are divided into First, Second and Third World categories.

1 *By contrasting the national profiles of countries*
Seeing this in terms of *quantitative* distinctions, for example,
wealth and military power, and *qualitative* distinctions, for
example, private ownership as against state control of all
industry. It is then possible to place some countries in the First
World and some in the Second World. Third World countries
are relatively poor and weak and follow policies of 'development'
which are based firmly in their own cultural tradition.

2 *By defining the relations between countries*
The rich and the powerful, with their client states, have
different relationships between and among themselves, than
with or among the poor and weak. In particular, the rich
and powerful intervene in the poor and weak to maintain
the Third World's continuing dependence on First or Second
World countries.

Discussion point
Refer to figure 6 for examples of countries which could fit into
the categories listed above.

3 *By examining differing concepts of change*
Within the First World, the stress is on limited change within
the existing system, while in the Second World, the stress is on
change following Karl Marx's five-fold categorization of world
epochs. The Third World borrows from both, producing what
might be described as modernizing nationalism.

Proletarian democracy
Broadly speaking the countries that can be considered as
proletarian democracies are those that are normally referred
to as 'communist'. However, 'communist' is a misnomer
because none of these countries claim to have achieved the
ideal, equal society of communism; rather they claim to have a
socialist democracy in which the majority (the *proletariat* or
working class) or their representatives, rule over the minority
who seek to overthrow the established system.
    It is difficult to isolate the basic features of proletarian
democracy because such political systems have come about
under different circumstances. The USSR and China became
proletarian democracies as a result of revolutions, whilst many

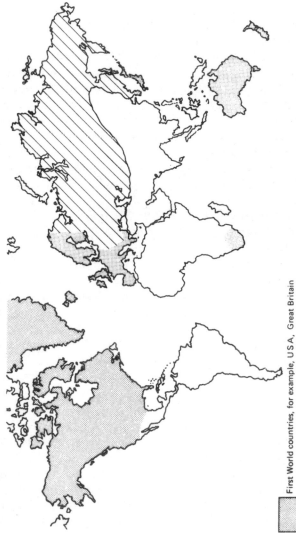

Figure 6 *The division of the world*

First World countries, for example, U S A, Great Britain

Second World countries, for example, U S S R, Bulgaria, Albania

Third World countries, for example, Brazil, Tanzania, India

of the satellite states of Eastern Europe became proletarian democracies after the Second World War. The feature of most pre-socialist societies is that of a lack of economic development – most were not industrialized when they took the road to proletarian democracy. This has always provided problems for Marxist thinkers because Marx claimed that it was only in a fully developed industrial state that the necessary polarization of classes existed to enable the socialist revolution to take place. Practical revolutionaries like Lenin, Trotsky, Mao Tse-tung and Castro have had to remould Marxist thinking to fit in with the political realities.

Probably the most important single change in Marx's theory and the key to understanding the proletarian democracies' idea of democracy is the change in the role of the political party. For Marx, a party was not necessary for the working class to develop the consciousness needed for revolution, but Lenin began the process by which the party was seen first as the vanguard of the proletariat and then as the repository of orthodoxy. The basic argument which proletarian democracies use to justify their claim to democracy can be stated in a series of propositions:

(a)   The revolution was created by the masses.
(b)   The party is the way in which the masses expressed themselves.
(c)   After the revolution the party represents the majority (the proletariat) and rules in their interest.

It is clear then, that the claim of the proletarian democracies to be democratic comes largely from the assertion that the party, which is virtually synonymous with the government, reflects the wishes of the majority. The party becomes the embodiment of the will of the masses, but is not necessarily open to all (especially in the USSR) for it must maintain its purity by admitting only those people who can prove themselves to be orthodox Marxist/Leninists. So there is little attempt to create a mass party.

Decision-making in proletarian democracies is also supposed to be a democratic feature – based on the ideas of 'democratic centralism'. At its simplest, this means that there is a flow upwards of information from the grass roots through the party to the leaders who then formulate policies which take account of grass-roots opinion; when these policies are formulated they are passed down the structure for comment and amended by the leaders in the light of these comments. When this has been done a final policy is produced which, it is expected, all of the party and people will adhere to. Some critics have noted that this democratic ideal has, in practice, become distorted, as party leaders may inhibit or positively discourage lower-level officials from questioning or commenting on the decisions of the leadership.

Many of the critics of proletarian democracies point to the apparent lack of the personal freedoms which are given so much emphasis in a liberal democracy – free speech, free assembly and so forth are severely limited. It should be remembered, however, that the extent of allowable opposition varies from one proletarian democracy to another. China is noticeably more willing to allow criticism than is the USSR. Such limitations are not a direct result of the constitutions of proletarian democracies, for such documents generally guarantee the rights of individuals, providing they do not endanger the state. It is clear that what constitutes a danger to the state is perceived differently in societies such as the USSR and the UK. Probably the best way to explain the restrictions on personal liberties is to add another proposition to the three given above;

(*d*) As the party represents the masses and their wishes, any person or group which criticizes the party or government is attacking the masses and so endangering the revolution.

Great publicity is given in the West to the oppression of minorities and dissident groups in many proletarian democracies, and especially to some of the very harsh treatment which is meted out to opposition groups. But such action is made more intelligible (if no less abhorrent) by the type of argument outlined in point (*d*) above. A recent refinement of this fourth proposition in the USSR has been that all thinking men realize that communism and the Russian state are the best form of social organization, so that anybody who opposes the state must be mentally unbalanced. This has led to some dissidents being committed to mental hospitals as being insane.

Another addition to these propositions is the lack of need for any opposition party: if the masses are already adequately represented by the Party, no other party is necessary; indeed it would be undemocratic as it would be representing reactionary forces who wished to weaken the position of the masses and return to capitalism. The result of the monopoly of legitimate political activity by the communist parties is that any elections that are held are fought out between members within the communist party, and not between members of different parties.

To the liberal democrat, the proletarian democracies' restricted personal liberty, lack of freedom of choice and acceptance of government activity is intolerable. Many commentators believe the proletarian democracies to be totalitarian in the same way that Nazi Germany was. They point to the total intrusion of the state into all aspects of life, the restriction of personal liberties and take these to be signs that the proletarian democracies are totalitarian. Although this view can be defended, it can also mislead, for the proletarian democracies claim that their restrictions now are to enable true democracy to come about eventually. When this occurs the state and all restrictions will disappear. The Nazis denied that democracy could even exist and said that inequalities were a natural feature of life. Whatever the merits of such an argument, it seems clear that the majority of people in the proletarian democracies (especially those which were created by revolutions) do accept the right of their governments to make decisions which affect them.

Third World democracy

Throughout the Third World there exist political systems which are greatly different from those of the liberal democracies. In many of these countries there is only one party; often opposition parties are not allowed to function at all. Certainly it needs to be re-emphasized at this point that most Third World countries would claim to have or to be pursuing some form of democracy, for democratic government is generally held to be 'good' government, however the tag is interpreted in practice.

Most countries in the Third World are ex-colonial, though there are a few which never actually lost their independence: Ethiopia and Liberia in Africa, Turkey, Iran and Thailand in Asia. Some Third World leaders modelled their new political systems on the Westminster or Washington forms of liberal democracy, others on the Moscow or Peking forms of proletarian democracy: all found that in due course they had to adapt their regimes in accordance with the traditions and cultural base of their individual societies.

Rapid decolonization followed the Second World War and during this period many newly emergent nations experimented with liberal democracy, for it had not escaped the notice of the educated that the hitherto successful nations, in terms of stable government and economic prosperity, were of this type. Yet the existence of proletarian democracies, first in Russia then in China after 1949, also had an impact in Third World countries. Particularly impressive, in practical terms, was the disciplined mass organization achieved by communist parties and in the case of the USSR, the rapid industrialization accomplished through five-year programmes. Many new leaders sought the quickest route to change their traditional, agriculturally-based societies into modern, industrialized states and the communist way provided a tempting alternative to the liberal–democratic way.

The choices open to new Third World leaders must be seen in the context of colonialism. Some metropolitan powers withdrew from colonial territories gracefully and bloodlessly, as the Americans did from the Philippines, while others left in the wake of bitter strife, such as the Dutch from Indonesia. Understandably, some leaders of newly emergent states wished to sever, or at least minimize, links with the ex-metropolitan power. Moreover, equating as they did the European and American colonial powers with capitalism, they became fiercely nationalistic and some took the socialist road.

Many new Third World nations have only been independent for thirty years or less and therefore actively pursue a policy of nation-building in order to achieve national unity. National unity is not easy to obtain, for even in some Western nations there are groups who claim the right to create separate nations or regions because they have little in common with the nation. The problem is compounded in Third World countries by the often arbitrary way in which boundaries were created, tribes were often split by such boundaries and nations formed with an unstable tribal and ethnic mix. In the United Kingdom there are strong movements for independence for Ulster, Scotland and Wales. In Spain the Basques continue to try to become an autonomous region.

Third World examples include the Eritrean separatists who strive for autonomy from Ethiopian rule, and Moluccan separatists who seek autonomy from Indonesian rule.

The initiation of political participation, even narrowly interpreted on Western lines as a mass electorate choosing representatives to govern, is not easily achieved in many Third World states. The organized intellectual élites who took the reins of power on independence found that their writ ran little beyond twenty miles of their capital. Elsewhere, age-old customs continued and central government's efforts to penetrate Western ideas of democracy and economic development were not readily received. Traditionally most Third World countries developed strong local government controlled by a local potentate, a tribal chief or even a family. Good central government was unobtrusive government, which hardly affected the daily lives of the subjects. When it did, it was generally unwelcome, signifying crisis, such as war, famine or taxation of one kind or another. For the mass of people, the notion of being consulted was an entirely bewildering one. It was even felt by some that a government was incapable if it did not feel confident enough to govern without asking the people, and should therefore make way for a government that did!

Western democratic norms of government; a two-party system and regular elections, have proved to be difficult to introduce and sustain in Third World countries. This inevitably raises the question of the relevance of the Westminster or Washington models operating in such apparently infertile soil. Many Western liberals look with disillusionment at the sequence of coups, and resorts to a strong-arm rule in so many newly independent countries. Such disillusionment is deepened with the realization that the Moscow and Peking models of proletarian democracy have been spreading recently. The 'bamboo curtain' now covers Vietnam and Laos and there is communist insurgency in Thailand and Malaysia. In Africa, Angola has been taken over by the Russian-backed MPLA. However, Malaysia, Singapore and the Philippines have managed to achieve some semblance of liberal democracy, though they operate under the threat of subversion and racial conflict – features of their regimes. Whatever type of democracy has been adopted by Third World countries it has been modified, of necessity, to accommodate the national characteristics of each state. Sometimes this mixture has produced an almost unrecognizable political system, or democracy has become merely a façade for oligarchical or one-party dominance.

Liberal democracy

The classical Greek model of 'direct democracy', as outlined in the introduction to this chapter, has an immediate appeal to those who equate true democracy with a high degree of public participation in government. However, in modern mass societies there is one overriding obstacle to the implementation of this mode of government. It is the difficulty of achieving a high level of involvement in government affairs. To overcome this, *representative democracy* has emerged as an adaptation which meets the needs of modern nation-states.

What, then, are the characteristics and basic assumptions of representative democracies? A government must rest on the consent of the majority of the governed, remain accountable to the electorate by operating through the machinery charged with continuous assessment of governmental objectives and work. This entails regular elections and the existence of institutionalized checks and balances.

Baron Montesquieu's doctrine of the separation of powers is designed to prevent the concentration of governmental power by dividing the main functions of government – the legislative, executive and judicial functions – into separate institutions controlled by different groups of officials. It has been noted that in the British context there is considerable fusion of these functions of government (separation of powers, page 35). For the same reason there is usually a division of the legislature into an upper and lower house (bicameralism), thereby creating the possibility of constructive delay if disagreement should arise on a point of legislation. Government is also divided at political levels between national and local authorities. Such arrangements are intended to bring friction, delay and the necessity for compromise into the operation of government. If government is to be carried out according to the tenets of democracy, the consultation must take place and a consensus achieved.

Within a democratic framework the election of representatives should be secret and uncoerced, with government operating the machinery in accordance with the law. Basic freedoms should be stated in the constitution, notably freedom of speech, religion, movement, assembly and the press.

Implicit in the liberal democratic ideal is a denial that there is an objective science of society or of morals; in the last resort truth is a matter for the individual in the sight of God and man. Therefore there can be no imposition of any creed, philosophy or ideology: all should be allowed to express their views within the law. Clearly, views of the truth will vary from time to time with governments remaining responsive to, and representative of, public opinion.

It has been noted that, when assessing advanced Western industrial societies, *pluralism* is the most prominent theory of democratic politics. Society is composed of many freely-formed, functioning, autonomous groups, each of which attempts to realize its own objectives through the machinery of state. In essence, democratic politics is viewed as a dynamic of *inputs* (interest group activity and elections) and government *outputs* (regulations and laws), as Figure 7 shows.

Figure 7 *The basis of democratic politics*

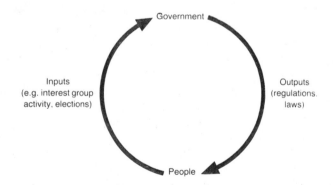

A liberal democracy is a qualified democracy. The authority of government rests on its ability to evaluate and process inputs from groups in society into acceptable outputs. Government performance can be measured by the proportions of consent, compliance and dissent present in society. Although tolerance of minority groups is a significant aspect of representative democracy, it is generally held that government should be in the interests of the nation as a whole. In the last instance, majority opinion should prevail.

It is one of the strengths of a theoretical position that it can be modified to encompass change. So within the broad pluralist explanation, three significant, historically-specific strands may be identified – conventional pluralism, neopluralism and the New Right.

Conventional pluralism

In essence this position emphasizes party competition, interest group activity, the separation of political and economic life (representative democracy and capitalist economics), and the neutrality of the government when operating the machinery of the state in response to inputs from social groups. A democratically stable society is achieved by establishing an equilibrium between societal inputs and governmental outputs. Government remains continually responsive to the wishes of its citizens individually and in groups – all of whom have *equal* access to decision-makers.

Neopluralism

Empirical evidence in the late 1960s and the 1970s punctured conventional pluralist theory. British party politics became markedly class-oriented and sectarian conflict grew in Northern Ireland. Problems arose in other liberal democracies – urban race riots and anti-Vietnam demonstrations developed in the USA, serious demonstrations and strikes occurred in France in 1968. This needs to be seen together with an intensification of criticism by élite theorists such as C. Wright Mills, who identified one controlling élite rather than a system of competing élites. All this seriously dented the explanatory properties of conventional pluralism with its emphasis on consensus politics. Neopluralists attempted to counter such deficiencies by emphasizing the *inequality of interest group input* and the heightened importance of professionals, such as top civil servants and board members of public corporations, in government. As society became more complex and government decisions more problematic then, it was claimed, decision-making came to rest more heavily on professionals in government departments and professionals from 'valued' interest groups, for example the TUC and the CBI. It was concluded that the relationship between technically/professionally able interest group personnel and responsive government officials raised the quality of problem-solving and therefore the legitimacy of government in terms of generating consent-maximizing outputs. At the same time, unrest was explained by the apparently reduced significance of voting and the frustrations of 'outsider' interest groups.

The New Right
The New Right is a development of the 1980s. In economic terms it stresses a free market system unfettered by state intervention. In political terms this variant is still within the broad pluralist tradition. New Right advocates do not accept that government can, or should, be responsive to all inputs from groups in society. Too many interest group inputs overload government and produce irresistible pressure to centralize decision-making and spend tax-payers' money. Moreover, an excessively 'cosy' relationship between government officials and outside interests can impair a government's ability to make objective decisions. Mrs Thatcher's administrations have exhibited certain New Right characteristics such as a steady privatization programme of certain public corporations, e.g. British Telecom, a reduction in the size of the Civil Service, and a distancing by the government in its dealings with the TUC and the CBI.

Democracy in Britain

As we have seen, the question 'Is Britain a democracy?' may best be answered by another question, 'What do you mean by democracy?' To most people, though, this would be seen merely as a discussion of semantics because it is generally recognized that Britain is a democracy. Many of the arguments used to support such a view are made elsewhere in this book and it may be pertinent here to draw some of the most important ones together and to show some of the limitations of this view. It is not our intention to imply that Britain is not a democracy, merely to reinforce the general argument that to see political activity in black and white terms is to over-simplify a very complex process.

Elements of democracy	*Limits to these elements*
i) The British electoral system provides for free choice between competing political parties.	These parties are composed of leaders whose social and economic background is not typical of the populace. The public have no say in the selection of the people offered as candidates. Strong parties limit the ability of the individual to win a seat in parliament as an independent.
ii) The electoral system provides strong and stable government.	Such government is bought at the expense of minority representation in parliament. The Liberal Party and others find it difficult to win seats and break the two-party domination.
	Governments in Britain rarely have the support of the majority of those who vote or those entitled to vote. Is strong government in such circumstances a good thing?
iii) Governments must be responsive to public opinion if they are to survive, hence the policies they follow are moderate and, usually, those that the public wants.	Evidence suggests that individual policies are less important to the electorate than overall party image. All governments follow policies, from time to time, which are unpopular and even extreme. Governments may refuse to implement some policies which it seems the majority of the public supports, for example, the restoration of the death penalty.

Elements of democracy	*Limits to these elements*
iv) The British government has to stand for periodic re-election, at least every five years.	The discretion of the Prime Minister can give the government an advantage in calling an election. Would fixed terms of office be a more democratic solution?
v) All adults over the age of 18 may vote and all over the age of 21 may stand as parliamentary candidates (with a few minor exceptions).	There are few limitations on these rights but not all votes are equally important because of unequal-sized constituencies and the many 'safe seats' which effectively take away any influence from many voters. Without party support a candidate stands almost no chance of winning an election. Parties are much more powerful than the committed individual.
vi) Any view, however extreme, can be voiced because of the right of free expression.	Such expression is limited by the existence of the laws of slander and libel. The press is subject to 'advice' through the 'D notice' system. More importantly the abstract right to free expression is not at all useful if access to the means of spreading such ideas is barred. Extreme groups and ordinary individuals find it difficult to gain coverage in the media for their views. Well-known individuals find no such difficulty.

Elements of democracy	*Limits to these elements*
vii) There is freedom of association.	This is true generally but there are occasions when this is limited, for example, picketing and demonstrating. Such limits are justified as being to protect the freedom of others.
viii) There is freedom from arbitrary arrest and equality in law.	This freedom is limited from time to time when it is thought that it is in the interests of the nation to do so, for example, during war time or as a result of terrorist bombing. This usually involved the suspension of *Habeas Corpus*, and the latest example of which is the Prevention of Terrorism Act 1976. As we have seen, the law does not always apply equally to all groups. Police discretion results in certain groups being more liable to arrest for certain offences.
ix) Separation of powers means that no individual or group can have too much power.	There is no total separation of powers in Britain so the possibility of one-group dominance still remains. Many would say that the cabinet or Prime Minister now wield overwhelming power in the British system by controlling parliament and the types of legislation presented. Government defeats are very rare; those that do occur, for example, the 1979 Labour Government, can in part be blamed on ineptitude.

Elements of democracy	*Limits to these elements*
x) There are still areas of private life where government will not legislate or interfere. Private morality is the concern only of the individual. It is usually left to individual MPs to introduce Private Members' Bills dealing with questions of morality. Such Bills have little chance of success unless they have government backing.	There are now few areas of life where government has not, at some stage, intervened. The family is increasingly seen as responsible to government and parents now have less discretion in raising their children, for example, Education Acts must be obeyed. Local government provides social services which some see as, at times, interfering with families. In general, governments are unwilling to venture too far into the field of morality but in almost all other areas their influence is felt.
xi) Democracy is concerned with open government.	Successive governments have argued that large areas of government activity should remain secret. The Official Secrets Act 1911 is seen by many as a gross restriction on open government. Increasingly government is keeping detailed information about some aspects of the life of individuals, much of this is secret and not available to the individual himself.

It can be seen, then, that democracy remains an ideal to aim for rather than an achieved end.

Exercise
What factors would it be necessary to look at to discover

whether a country was democratic? Which countries would qualify under this definition?

Conclusion

It can be seen that democracy, like many other concepts, is not amenable to a single, simple definition. It is possible to point to various alternative interpretations which can legitimately be advanced as acceptable descriptions. A continuing strand throughout this book has been to show that political activity is a complex and varied phenomenon which cannot be described in black and white terms. All of the concepts considered are problematic in the sense that there is no one 'correct' definition or description; some of the alternative descriptions have been put forward in preceding pages.

Although the concepts have been presented as being separate it should be clear that they are, in reality, inextricably interlinked. The concept of liberal democracy, for example, involves certain notions as to the nature, and desirability, of order, rights, justice, representation and so on. To understand any political system it is essential to know what interpretations are placed on such notions. Adopting this type of approach we might conclude that liberal democracy, as a system, places great stress on rights, sometimes to the detriment of order. Dictatorships tend to put order above all other considerations.

Such a method of analysis is of great use to the student of politics, for it enables him to penetrate the surface of a political system, to see past the institutions to the essence of how the system operates, and to see what is considered to be truly important.

Essay questions

1 'In Britain today democracy is at risk; political decisions are no longer made under the spotlight of public debate, but behind the scenes where pressure groups operate.' Evaluate this statement. (AEB Specimen Question 1986) *Read Chapter 5 before attempting this question.*
2 'Political activity involves a delicate balance between consensus and conflict: too much of either destroys the political system.' Comment. (Cambridge, Summer 1982)

3   What are the respective merits, if any, of Marxist and
     pluralist analyses of power in Britain? (Cambridge,
     Summer 1983)
4   Are 'democracy' and 'majority rule' the same thing?
     (Oxford, Summer 1985)
5   What is meant when it is said that Britain is a pluralistic
     state? (London, January 1980)
6   Marxists claim that the institutions of the state can never
     be politically neutral. Discuss this Marxist contention.
     (London, January 1983)

Short-answer questions
1   Distinguish between political and legal sovereignty.
     (London, January 1981)
2   Define the concept of 'limited government'. (London,
     January 1982)
3   What are the essential elements of parliamentary govern-
     ment? (London, January 1983)
4   Define 'political toleration'. (London, January 1985)

Glossary

This glossary contains short definitions of some of the concepts which occur in the text. Such definitions provide only an outline of the concept and the student is referred to the relevant chapter for a fuller discussion. As these concepts are not amenable to a single 'correct' definition the reader should treat the following definitions purely as working definitions. Words in bold print in the glossary have a separate entry.

Authority is the ability to get people to do things because they think an individual, or group, has the **right** to tell them what to do.

Compliance is the submission by a person, or group, to the commands of those who govern.

Conflict exists whenever people, or groups, disagree over which goals to pursue and the methods and timing to be adopted.

Consent involves the agreement by an individual, or group, that the political decisions made by those who govern, and the leaders themselves are **legitimate**.

A **constitution** is the principles, rules and conventions by which a state is governed.

Democracy originally meant a system of government based on the participation of all qualified citizens in decision-making. It is now usually used to describe a political system in which the individual is involved in choosing a representative from competing political parties, or sometimes, from one party.

Dissent involves disagreement with the process by which leaders are chosen or impose themselves, and/or the decisions they make.

Freedom is the ability to act in a manner unrestrained by external pressures, or to refrain from such action if it is so desired.

Influence is the ability to affect decisions through persuasion.

Justice is the idea that people's relationships with one another should be based on some understanding of fairness and impartiality.

Laws are the formally enacted rules of society by which citizens are bound.

Legitimacy is the idea that those who govern have the rightful **authority** to do so.

Liberties are the kind of actions considered acceptable by a particular society. They are closely linked with **freedom** and **rights**.

Order involves a situation in which an individual is able to make calculations with the exception that society will remain sufficiently stable for these plans to be fulfilled. Without order society is impossible.

Politics has at its root conflict between individuals, or groups, about how problems are to be resolved and the methods to be used. It is often used to describe the processes of decision-making at national and local levels.

Power is the ability to get things done, to make others do what you want – even if they do not want to do it.

Pressure is the application, by groups, of organized persuasion with the intention of affecting decision-making.

Representation is the relationship between a person chosen to protect and promote the interests of an individual, or group, having given him the **authority** to do so.

Responsibility is the idea that those in **power** remain answerable to those who are governed.

Rights are entitlements which, at the highest level, may be associated with membership of mankind, natural rights. Civil rights are those conferred by membership of a particular society.

Sovereignty is supreme **power**. It resides in that body which has the ultimate decision-making **power**.

Index